EMPOWERMENT AND SAMAYA

What They Didn't Tell You

RANGJUNG YESHE BOOKS • WWW.RANGJUNG.COM

PADMASAMBHAVA: *Treasures from Juniper Ridge* • *Advice from the Lotus-Born* • *Dakini Teachings* • *Following in Your Footsteps: The Lotus-Born Guru in Nepal* • *Following in Your Footsteps: The Lotus-Born Guru in India* • *The Lotus-Born Guru in Tibet*

PADMASAMBHAVA AND JAMGÖN KONGTRÜL: *The Light of Wisdom, Vol. 1, Vol. 2, Vol. 3, Secret, Vol. 4 & Vol. 5*

PADMASAMBHAVA, CHOKGYUR LINGPA, JAMYANG KHYENTSE WANGPO, TULKU URGYEN RINPOCHE, ORGYEN TOBGYAL RINPOCHE, & OTHERS *Dispeller of Obstacles* • *The Tara Compendium* • *Powerful Transformation* • *Dakini Activity*

YESHE TSOGYAL: *The Lotus-Born*

DAKPO TASHI NAMGYAL: *Clarifying the Natural State*

TSELE NATSOK RANGDRÖL: *Mirror of Mindfulness* • *Heart Lamp* • *Empowerment and Samaya*

CHOKGYUR LINGPA: *Ocean of Amrita* • *The Great Gate* • *Skillful Grace* • *Great Accomplishment* • *Guru Heart Practices*

TRAKTUNG DUDJOM LINGPA: *A Clear Mirror*

JAMGÖN MIPHAM RINPOCHE: *Gateway to Knowledge, Vol. 1, Vol. 2, Vol. 3, & Vol. 4*

TULKU URGYEN RINPOCHE: *Blazing Splendor* • *Rainbow Painting* • *As It Is, Vol. 1 & Vol. 2* • *Vajra Speech* • *Repeating the Words of the Buddha* • *Dzogchen Deity Practice* • *Vajra Heart Revisited*

ADEU RINPOCHE: *Freedom in Bondage*

KHENCHEN THRANGU RINPOCHE: *Crystal Clear*

CHÖKYI NYIMA RINPOCHE: *Bardo Guidebook* • *Collected Works of Chökyi Nyima Rinpoche, Vol. 1 & Vol. 2*

TULKU THONDUP: *Enlightened Living*

ORGYEN TOBGYAL RINPOCHE: *Life & Teachings of Chokgyur Lingpa* • *Straight Talk* • *Sublime Lady of Immortality*

DZIGAR KONGTRÜL RINPOCHE: *Uncommon Happiness*

TSOKNYI RINPOCHE: *Fearless Simplicity* • *Carefree Dignity*

MARCIA BINDER SCHMIDT: *Dzogchen Primer* • *Dzogchen Essentials* • *Quintessential Dzogchen* • *Confessions of a Gypsy Yogini* • *Precious Songs of Awakening Compilation*

ERIK PEMA KUNSANG: *Wellsprings of the Great Perfection* • *A Tibetan Buddhist Companion* • *The Rangjung Yeshe Tibetan-English Dictionary of Buddhist Culture & Perfect Clarity*

EMPOWERMENT AND SAMAYA

What They Didn't Tell You

Padmasambhava, Jamgön Kongtrül Rinpoche, Tsele Natsok Rangdröl, Kyabje Tulku Urgyen Rinpoche, Orgyen Tobgyal Rinpoche, & Lama Putsi

Translated by
Erik Pema Kunsang

Edited and Compiled by
Marcia Binder Schmidt

Rangjung Yeshe Publications
526 Entrada Drive, Apt. 201
Novato, CA 94949 USA

Address emails to:
Rangjung Yeshe Publications
C/O above

www.rangjung.com
www.lotustreasure.com

First paperback edition published in 2024
Printed in the United States of America

Distributed to the book trade by:
Publishers Group West/Ingram

ISBN 13: 978-1-7357345-5-2 (pbk)

Title: *Empowerment and Samaya*
Sub. What They Didn't Tell You
Padmasambhava, Tsele Natsok Rangdrol, Chokgyur
Lingpa, Jamgön Kongtrül Lodrö Thaye, Khakyab Dorje,
Tersey Tulku, Kyabje Tulku Urgyen Rinpoche, Orgyen
Tobgyal Rinpoche, and Lama Putsi

1. Vajrayana—Tradition of Pith Instructions
2. Buddhism—Tibet

Contents

Foreword

Marcia Binder Schmidt

Empowerment is a vast topic in which there are so many different levels. Most people go to empowerments to receive a blessing. They convince themselves that this is a good enough reason to take the trouble to attend. However, as practitioners, we need to look more closely, as empowerment is the way to ripen our being and lead us to realization. We need to understand not only what we are getting ourselves into, but how empowerment actually brings us to accomplishment. We also need to know to what we are really committing and pledging.

Empowerments are multifaceted and complex. Each aspect is finely orchestrated and entails a realized, compassionate, bestower of the empowerment, a dedicated student, proper ritual objects, and tantric substances. Before we even enter the place where the empowerment is to be given, there are activities that the lama imparting the empowerment needs to accomplish. These include all the preparations for the ritual with the necessary practices, and the proper and correct arrangement of the shrine.

Then there are the prerequisites that the student needs to fulfill. Usually, the practitioner has made the request to receive the empowerment for the particular practice that he or she intends to do, or perhaps is already engaged in. Motivation should be of the exalted type in that the student respects the teacher and the teaching, and vows to do the practice.

To give a bird's-eye view into the intricacy of empowerments, I have included several empowerment manuals in this book: two in the main body and two in the Appendices. The authors are Khakyab Dorje, the fifteenth Karmapa, Tersey Tulku, Lerab Lingpa, and Chokgyur Lingpa, whose manual was revealed as a terma. These manuals elucidate the intricate manner in which empowerments are approached and carried out. They highlight the responsibilities of both master and disciple. For additional reference, other chapters included here give scriptural source material replete with commentaries by past and current teachers explaining the nature of empowerment and samayas.

Then regarding samayas, the vows we take on as part of our commitment to Secret Mantra, what always surprises me, even with older, experienced dharma students, is how little we understand about samayas. Not only are there samayas in the context of empowerment, there are samayas for receiving different levels of teachings from the same teacher. The seemingly easiest samayas to understand are the fourteen root samayas, which are the most basic and clear commitments we make.

The first three are: to not go against our teacher, to not go against the dharma, and to not go against our dharma brothers and sisters. Orgyen Tobgyal Rinpoche criticizes that Westerners can seemingly keep the first but rarely the third. In his experience, Western students reveal little regard for their dharma siblings when they undermine them to him. Are we so oblivious to the major negative consequences we perpetuate?

Moreover, teachers are reluctant to openly discuss samayas prior to giving an empowerment or a profound teaching, another point Orgyen Tobgyal Rinpoche makes. Due to this lack of forthrightness, our ignorance is not completely our fault alone. Unfortunately, there is a way that some teachers and students use samaya as a weapon to try to suppress, control, and admonish others, when they do not really understand samayas themselves. With a wish to dispel such wrong views and educate students, I have compiled this book that clearly explains both these topics. Hence, the book you now hold in your hands—*Empowerment and Samaya, What They Didn't Tell You*—will reveal all you have not been told. For all these reasons, it is crucial that we closely study texts such as these to gain an understanding of the various categories of empowerment, and what samaya really is. Through this, we will arrive at a clear understanding of what entering through empowerment demands of us and what exactly it means to keep or break, the samaya commitments.

As always, it is necessary that we investigate for ourselves if we are keeping the samayas or not. Certainly, some samayas, such as the Dzogchen (Great Perfection) samayas, are extremely hard to keep, because any time that we stray from the view we've broken samaya. But on a day-to-day basis what do we really need to adhere to, and how should we do it? This can all be learned. Finally, there are also explanations and practices on how to mend and purify broken or damaged samayas.

Empowerment and Samaya has come into existence due to the translations of Erik Pema Kunsang. I have had the good fortune of receiving clarifications by many great masters, such as Kyabje Tulku Urgyen Rinpoche, Orgyen Tobgyal Rinpoche, and Lama Putsi. My gratitude knows no boundaries. Thanks go to Owsley Brown III for sponsorship, to anonymous for editing, to Joan Olson for typesetting, and to Deidre Goldberg for proofreading. I accept responsibility for any faults and apologize in advance for any mistakes.

May we overcome all damages and transgressions and join all together in whichever buddhafield we aspire to.

May the aspirations. activities, and precious teachings of Sonam Gyalsten Rinpoche flourish and continue to benefit all beings throughout all times and for aeons to come.

Offered by Dechen Gyalmo

Introduction

Kyabje Tulku Urgyen Rinpoche

There are the ripening empowerments, the liberating oral instructions, and the reading transmissions, which are the support. Concerning the ripening empowerments, 'ripening' means that your body is ripened into the deity, your speech is ripened into mantra, and your mind is ripened into samadhi.

In the Vajrayana teachings the main empowerments are known as the four empowerments. The first, the vase empowerment, relates to Mahayoga. In Anu Yoga there are two parts: through your own body and through the body of another. The empowerment through your own body is called the secret empowerment, and the empowerment through the body of another is called the wisdom-knowledge empowerment. Finally, the fourth is called the word [of primordial purity] empowerment. By means of these four empowerments—which are also referred to as elaborate, unelaborate, very unelaborate, and extremely unelaborate—empowerment is conferred. The basis of all Vajrayana teachings is the four empowerments.

Everything is included within the practices of the four empowerments. The vase empowerment is given best by means of a mandala of colored sand, of a painted canvas, or at least of heaps of grains. After having received the vase empowerment, one practices the development stage. Next is the Anu Yoga path, to which both the secret empowerment and the wisdom-knowledge empowerment belong.

In accordance with the four empowerments, appearance-emptiness is the vase empowerment; clarity-emptiness is the secret empowerment; and bliss-emptiness is the wisdom-knowledge empowerment. In Dzogchen's empty awareness there is no place at all to put the mind. Empty awareness is what needs to be acknowledged. In the empty clarity, there is the clarity side, and in the empty bliss, the bliss side. In empty appearance, there is somewhat a place for mind. Utilizing the words, come to the understanding that empty awareness is the awareness that knows the empty, stripped to nakedness.

All the different vehicles teach about emptiness, but the vase empowerment doesn't really purify the subtle dualistic fixation. Neither does the secret empowerment, nor the knowledge empowerment. It is only right at the borderline between the third and the fourth empowerments that one actually deals with subtle dualistic fixation. The precious word empowerment is the great accomplishment of the resultant Ati Yoga.

In the secret empowerment, one visualizes the buddha mandala of one's own body. One's body, since the beginning, is actually the buddha mandala itself, and simply reminding oneself of that, one does the practice. In the secret empowerment, one receives the bodhichitta and drinks that. Through this, one's obscurations and habitual tendencies are purified.

The practices connected to both [secret and wisdom-knowledge empowerments] utilize the channels (nadi), winds (prana), and essences (bindu), which are visualized as having the nature of dakas and dakinis. For the secret empowerment, one's own body is the upaya, skillful means. Then, for the wisdom-knowledge practice, one uses the body of another person. These [two] practices are also called 'the upper gate of the six yogas' and 'the lower gate of sporting in the three realms.' These practices both belong to Anu Yoga. They are the second and third empowerments.

There are actual substances in the vase, secret, wisdom-knowledge, and word empowerments. To bestow the four empowerments, the [respective] substances are necessary; it is not appropriate to do so without them.

After the completion of the practices related to the three first empowerments, comes the fourth empowerment, which is the precious word empowerment of Ati Yoga. The precious word empowerment introduces the nature of mind through just a word or a sentence. That is why it is called the precious word empowerment. It is an empowerment into the mandalas of what is already abiding in oneself, in one's own mind, abiding as the ground and as the manifest mandala of the ground. It introduces the mandala of mind that is the primordially pure essence and the spontaneously present nature, the outer mandala of the all-encompassing peaceful and wrathful sugatas that are abiding as the ground. Through this empowerment, one realizes that. This is the fruition empowerment.

With receiving the vase empowerment, one recognizes that all the world has the nature of deity, a divine nature. In Secret Mantra Vajrayana, you see that there is nothing other than deity, mantra, and samadhi. Whatever is seen has the nature of deity, all sounds have the nature of mantra, and all thoughts have the nature of enlightened mind. Recognizing that to be as it is, is the intent of Mahayoga, which is pointed out in the vase empowerment with its three aspects corresponding to body, speech, and mind.

If you were to wonder, "What is the secret empowerment?" at best, it includes the bodhichitta nectar from Padmasambhava, or from the great masters of the lineage. The white and red elements are dissolved into the skull-cup's contents. This empowers one's speech. By means of its taste, one's nature will ripen into sambhogakaya. The moment you drink it, your nadis are the Vajra Body, your pranas are the Vajra Speech and your bindus are the Vajra Mind.

Both the secret empowerment and the wisdom-knowledge empowerment belong to the Anu Yoga path. These empowerments for the Anu Yoga path [are related to practices for] the upper and lower gates: [those associated with] the upper gate are called the Six Vajra Doctrines, while [the practices associated with] the lower gate is called the 'sporting of the three realms.' For the secret empowerment, you receive the empowerment by drinking the bodhichitta essence. This is for the upper gate. For the lower gate, 'the sporting of the three realms,' isn't it the case that the male disciples, who are the dakas, receive the icon of a dakini? If you are a female, a dakini disciple, you receive a vajra in your hand, which symbolizes the daka.

'Sporting in the three realms' means that all three realms (the three levels of existence), have their source in the lower gate, within the central channel. "Sporting" means to overturn or churn up from the depths of samsara through this path by descending, reverting, retaining, and spreading. The purpose of that is the wisdom-knowledge empowerment.

Finally, there is the precious word empowerment whereby, in Dzogchen, the example for primordial purity is the showing of a crystal, which is also called the 'mirror of Vajrasattva.' For the word empowerment itself, the master shows a peacock feather. The eye on the peacock feather has natural colors; nobody painted them. They are uncreated. According to the New Schools, one shows a mirror. There are four lines from the *Barchey Kunsel* empowerment that illustrate the word empowerment:

> Like a reflection appearing on the surface of a
>   mirror,
> There is no thing to find, yet it appears vividly.
> By conferring the empowerment of an enlightened
>   mind into your mind,
> May all your thought activity be self-arising and
>   self-liberating.

When a reflection appears in a mirror, we need not imagine it is there, because it is vividly perceived. In the same way, we need not imagine basic wakefulness; it is naturally present. This is the example. When conferring the empowerment of enlightened mind, the empowerment of nondual wakefulness, [the result is] that your thought activity becomes self-arising and self-liberating. All thought activity occurs as the expression of rigpa. By recognizing their source, they dissolve back into the state of rigpa itself. Thoughts only happen as an expression of your essence, not from anywhere else. They don't arise from the five elements, from the five sense organs, from flesh, blood, temperature, heat, or breath in your body—not at all. They are only the expression of the primordially pure essence. Once you recognize your essence to be primordial purity, the thoughts that arise from yourself dissolve back into yourself within the expanse of your nature. They don't go anywhere else. They are self-arising and self-liberating. If you don't know your own essence, then what arises from yourself does not dissolve within yourself, but instead goes straying within the six realms of sentient beings.

Here, the key point is that the dualistic mind takes place as the expression of rigpa. Once you recognize rigpa, the thinking or display of thoughts loses all power and simply dissolves into the expanse of rigpa. This the basic reason to recognize mind-essence. Where does the thought occur from? Only from the display of your own nature. It doesn't come from any other source. Even if you were to look into that for a billion years, you would never see a thought arise out of earth, water, fire, or wind. There are vacuities in the body, blood, heat, and so forth, but these aspects do not give rise to thoughts. Thoughts do not arise from perceived objects, whether forms, sounds, smells, tastes, or textures. We have the five sense objects and the five sense organs in-between. A corpse also has these. It has eyes, but it does not see. It has ears, but it does not hear. It has a tongue, but it does not taste. It has a nose, but it does not smell. It has a body, but it does not feel. A corpse notices nothing. Isn't the basis for every experience your own mind, that which knows?

That which knows is, in essence, empty. It is cognizant by nature, and its capacity is unobstructed. One should recognize and know that this is how your essence is. Thoughts arise from yourself and dissolve into yourself. It is not that they arise from yourself and dissolve somewhere else. Thoughts arise from yourself and, if you recognize their source, they dissolve into yourself as well. So, what is recognized when we say 'recognize'? It is seeing empty cognizance, unobstructed, when you look. This is the real condition, the natural state of the three kayas. Realize the real condition, how it is, not just how it seems. The seeming way is our normal rigid, fixating thoughts. Upon recognizing the real state, the seeming way vanishes. These are the two aspects: the real and the seeming. The real is the essence; the seeming is thoughts. Once you recognize the real state, the seeming way vanishes without a trace. It collapses, dissolves, and vanishes. That's the practice.

Our essence is identified as the three kayas. Once you are stable in that, it is 100% certain that you will not have to flounder around any longer in samsara. This real state is, in itself, empty dharmakaya. Its cognizant quality is sambhogakaya. Its unconfined unity is nirmanakaya. This identity of the indivisible three kayas is called the 'essence body,' or svabhavikakaya. In this way, don't you have these three kayas right in the palm of your own hand? Do you have to seek them out somewhere else? This is the pith instruction called the Great Perfection, which is introduced by way of the precious word empowerment.

The Ripening Empowerments

Tsele Natsok Rangdrol[1]

THE RIPENING EMPOWERMENTS

Regarding your questions about the meaning and definition of obtaining empowerment, my reply will be accompanied by quotations from the tantras and arranged under two headings: general and specific.

Entering the door to the teachings of Secret Mantra Vajrayana depends upon two things: ripening and liberation. Unless you first obtain the ripening empowerments, you are not authorized to hear even a single verse of the tantras, statements and instructions. [Unauthorized] people who engage in expounding on and listening to the tantras will not only fail to receive blessings; they will create immense demerit from divulging the secrecy of these teachings. A person who has not obtained empowerment may pretend to practice the liberating instructions but, instead of bringing accomplishment, the practice will create obstacles and countless other defects. This is mentioned in the Buddha Skull Tantra:

> As a lute cannot be played without strings,
> Though all other parts may be present,
> The person who lacks empowerment
> Will not be successful in the practice of mantra
> and meditation.

The *Tantra of the Heart Mirror of Vajrasattva* further states:

13

Just as a boatman without oars
Cannot cross to the opposite bank of a river,
There will be no accomplishment without the
    support of empowerment.

The shortcomings of failing to obtain empowerment have
been mentioned in countless such ways. Regarding the ad-
vantages of receiving empowerment, the *Tantra of the Heart
Mirror of Vajrasattva* says:

Having fully obtained all the empowerments,
The entire Secret Mantra is accomplished without
    hardship.

The *Tantra of the Brilliant Expanse* further says:

The noble child who has obtained empowerment
Accomplishes all wishes in this life,
And attains true enlightenment in the next.

Innumerable other similar quotations exist.

The basic materials or seeds for the empowerments in question are already spontaneously present within one's own nature. The master's blessings and the symbolic indications [of
the words, gestures and implements used during the ritual]
provide the circumstances for their growth. As an analogy,
consider the enthronement ceremony of a universal monarch. The person enthroned must unmistakenly be of royal
birth, and yet until he is established on the throne he is only
called 'prince,' never 'king.' Once he has been enthroned
and has been conferred with rulership of the kingdom, he
becomes king in actuality.

Similarly, while the seeds of the four empowerments are

primordially present in the disciple's nature, the original wisdom will not be actualized until these seeds have been ripened through empowerment. Once the disciple embarks upon the path of ripening and liberation, the wisdom of his own nature will be actualized. This is described in the *Subsequent Tantra of the Bathing Elephant:*

> The mind essence of sentient beings is the
>   luminous nature of self-awareness,
> The unfabricated awakened state, a continuity that
>   is spontaneously present.
> Once you embark on the path of ripening and
>   liberating this luminous nature,
> You clearly perceive the fruition within your own
>   being.

I shall now explain empowerment in terms of its essential identity, etymological definition, categories, and purpose.

The *Tantra that Embodies the Four Rivers of Empowerment* describes the essential identity of empowerment:

> It purifies, ripens, and refines your being,
> Infuses you with innate wakefulness,
> And implants in your mind-stream [the seed of]
>   the fruition
> Of attaining the indestructible thirteenth bhumi.

Thus, empowerment is the king of all methods that cause the original wisdom inherent in yourself to naturally manifest.

The etymological definition of empowerment is like this: Formerly your body, speech, and mind followed deluded habitual tendencies and possessed no independent power. The method that now provides you with natural authority over the indivisible state of the four kayas is called 'empowerment.'

The Sanskrit word for empowerment, *abhishencha*, literally means 'to cleanse defilements,' in the sense that the power of the four empowerments removes the obscurations of body, speech, mind, and cognition. The Sanskrit word *abhisheka* is also used, meaning 'to instill with an entitlement.' What kind of entitlement is one instilled with? The vase empowerment entitles or authorizes you to visualize your body as a deity, the secret empowerment to practice the channels and energies, the wisdom-knowledge empowerment to practice coemergent bliss and emptiness, and the precious word empowerment to practice the unity beyond concepts.

The Sanskrit word *abhisiddhi* is also used, meaning 'to be accomplished' or 'to be ripened.' How is one ripened? The vase empowerment ripens the physical aggregates, elements, and sense-factors into a deity; the secret empowerment ripens the voice and the inhalation, exhalation, and abiding of the breath into the nature of mantra; the wisdom-knowledge empowerment ripens the bindu essences into great bliss and all sensation into coemergent wisdom; and the word empowerment ripens all that appears and exists into all-encompassing purity, the all-pervasive continuity of dharmakaya.

The categories of empowerment differ according to the various sections of tantras. To quote the *Wisdom Bindu:*

> Empowerment with water and empowerment
> with crown
> Are described in the Kriya tantras.
> The vajra, bell, and also name [empowerments]
> Are clearly explained in the Charya tantras.

The empowerment of no return
Is elucidated in the Yoga tantras.

According to the Kriya tantras, the disciple is rendered a suitable vessel by the water empowerment, the crown empowerment, and also by means of the knowledge entrustment, etc. In the Charya tantras, the additional empowerments of vajra, bell, and name—which together [with the two above] are called the five knowledge empowerments—are conferred on the disciple. The Yoga tantras include an additional empowerment called the irreversible master empowerment, or the empowerment for accomplishing vajra conduct. A general method for bestowing these empowerments is used by the Sarma and Nyingma schools of Secret Mantra.

Inner Secret Mantra's special Anuttara Tantra tradition for conferring the complete four empowerments also does not fundamentally differ from the teachings of the Sarma and Nyingma schools [regarding the outer tantras], although there are numerous minor variations within the four. According to the Sarma schools, the empowerments of Chakrasamvara, Hevajra, and Guhyasamaja are for the most part alike.

The Kalachakra system teaches that the water of the initial vase empowerment is for purifying the defilements of the five elements, accomplishing the siddhis of the five consorts, and attaining the first bhumi. The crown empowerment is for purifying the defilement of the five aggregates, accomplishing the siddhis of the five buddhas, and attaining the second bhumi. These two empowerments purify the obscurations of the body and implant the seed for attaining the Vajra Body.

Similarly, the tiara-streamer empowerment is for purifying the defilements of the ten winds, accomplishing the siddhis of the ten consorts, and attaining the third bhumi. The vajra and bell empowerments are for purifying the defilements of the right and left channels, accomplishing the siddhi of the male and female chief figures, and attaining the fourth bhumi. These two empowerments purify the obscurations of speech and implant the seed of Vajra Speech in your being.

The empowerment of yogic discipline is for purifying the defilements of the eight consciousnesses, the sense faculties and sense objects, accomplishing the siddhis of the male and female bodhisattvas, and attaining the fifth bhumi. The name empowerment is for purifying the defilements of 'doer and deed' [subject and object], accomplishing the siddhis of the male and female wrathful ones, and attaining the sixth bhumi. These two empowerments purify the obscurations of mind and implant the capacity to attain the state of the Vajra Mind.

The permission-blessing and supportive ritual are for purifying the defilements that obscure the nature of original wakefulness, accomplishing the siddhi of Vajrasattva and consort, the lord of the family, attaining the seventh bhumi, and connecting with the fruitional state of vajra wisdom. These seven empowerments[2] are called the 'seven empowerments to initiate immature beings,' and it is taught that the person who has obtained them becomes a lay practitioner (*upasika*) of Secret Mantra.

Following that, the vase empowerment implants the capacity to attain the eighth bhumi and validates one as a novice (*shramanera*) of Secret Mantra. Through the secret empowerment one attains the ninth bhumi and becomes a fully ordained practitioner (*bhikshu*) of Secret Mantra. By means of the wisdom-knowledge empowerment one attains the tenth and eleventh bhumis. Through the fourth empowerment one attains the twelfth bhumi and becomes a great lord of beings. Thus, as the Kalachakra system teaches, the empowerments guide you through progressive stages.

All the other tantras divide the vase empowerment into the five knowledge empowerments followed by the empowerment of the conduct of a vajra master. Then follow, one after the other, the secret empowerment, the wisdom-knowledge empowerment, and the word empowerment. There are numerous systems of classifying empowerments.

According to the Nyingma school of Secret Mantra, there are two ways of dividing empowerments: either into the 'four rivers of empowerment,' corresponding to their origin; or into the 'four steps of empowerment,' corresponding to their method of bestowal. The four rivers of empowerment are:

- the empowerment of the scripture of teachings,
- the empowerment of the yidam deity,
- the empowerment of the learned pandita, and
- the empowerment of the expression of awareness.

The four steps of empowerment are the vase, secret, wisdom-knowledge, and word empowerments.

The subdivisions of each of these are described in the scriptural system of the *Magical Display of the Peaceful and Wrathful Ones*:

> Perform the empowerments of the crown, the tiara,
> The rosary, the armor, the banner,

The mudra, the parasol, the vase,
The food and drink, and the five essential
    components.

These are the ten outer benefitting empowerments. They are followed by the empowerments for the abilities of expounding, learning, sadhana practice, engaging in various activities, and acting as a vajra master. These are called the five inner enabling empowerments. All fifteen are subdivisions of the vase empowerment.

Following these, the secret empowerment, the wisdom-knowledge empowerment, and the empowerment of the indivisible great bliss are bestowed. These three are known as the three profound empowerments. Thus, there is a total of eighteen different empowerments.

The scripture called the *Eight Sadhana Teachings of the Assemblage of Sugatas*[3] divides empowerments into two categories: the special wisdom empowerment and the general compassion empowerment.

The special wisdom empowerment includes twenty-six empowerments:

- The eight empowerments based on the outer, indicating mandala of material substance, which upwardly embodies Kriya and Charya;[4]
- The nine empowerments, based on the inner 725 deities, which bestow the complete blessings of Mahayoga and Anu Yoga;
- The three empowerments of complete bodhichitta, based on the secret union of the father and mother aspects, for quickly traversing the paths and bhumis; and

- The six empowerments of the entire Ati of royal anointment, based on the innermost thatness mandala of self-aware wisdom.

The thirteen general compassion empowerments include the eight enabling empowerments of the all-encompassing teachings, and the five benefitting empowerments.

All these add up to thirty-nine empowerments, while the detailed subdivisions amount to 237 different empowerments.

According to the root text of the teaching cycle of *The Embodiment of the Guru's Realization* (*Lama Gongpa Düpa*),[5] the great ripening empowerment scripture entitled *the Heart Mirror,* the empowerment categories include:

- The outer vase empowerment in ten parts: the five knowledge empowerments and the five supportive empowerments;
- The inner empowerment of the all-encompassing teachings of the vajra king, in 117 parts;
- The secret empowerment of the vajra master, in thirty-four parts;
- The quality empowerment of the offering articles of precious accomplishment, in twenty-five parts;
- The activity empowerment of the attendants acting to tame beings, in 21 parts; and
- The seven empowerments of permission-blessing for the complete entrustment of the teachings.

Thus, there is a total of 213 parts.

According to the system of the grand empowerment of the *Scripture of the Great Assemblage* (*Düpa Do*), the chief of all the empowerments of the Nyingma school and the general empowerment of the nine gradual vehicles,[6] there are:

- The preliminary sixteen major supreme empowerments by means of the chief deity Vajrapani, indivisible from Vajrasattva, with twelve other retinue deities in the mandala. These purify misdeeds and obscurations and lead one away from the abodes of the lower realms.
- The vehicle of gods and humans of the higher realms discloses eleven mandalas and 123 empowerments.
- The vehicle of the shravakas has five mandalas and thirty-nine empowerments.
- The vehicle of the pratyekabuddhas has four mandalas and forty-five empowerments.
- The bodhisattva vehicle of aspiration and application has ten mandalas and fifty-three empowerments.
- The vehicle of Kriya has six mandalas and sixty-two empowerments.
- The vehicle of Ubhaya[7] has one mandala and twenty-eight empowerments.
- The vehicle of Yoga has the twofold mandala of Vajradhatu and ninety-nine empowerments.
- The vehicle of Mahayoga, of the unexcelled Secret Mantra, has the two aspects of peaceful and wrathful: the peaceful has six mandalas and 362 empowerments, while the wrathful has six mandalas and 640 empowerments.
- The vehicle of scripture Anu Yoga has eleven mandalas and 855 empowerments.
- The vehicle of Ati Yoga of the Great Perfection has one mandala and eighteen empowerments of the expression of awareness.

Serving as the support for all of the above is the longevity empowerment of accomplishment, with one mandala and fifty-eight empowerments. In short, without counting the different entrances to the mandala of *The Great Assemblage (Düpa Do),* tradition establishes that there are, in all, fifty-four mandalas of colored powder and fifty-five mandalas of three components, in which dwell 1,980 deities. The total number of empowerments amounts to 2,440.

The different categories of empowerment belonging to either the Old or New Schools of Secret Mantra are merely subdivisions of the four empowerments. They are not individual components of a complete structure consisting of the preliminary steps of preparation, the accomplishing and offerings of the main part, and the concluding ritual actions. The precise number of these categories differs greatly among the various empowerment texts of the Sarma and Nyingma schools. How can one possibly establish a fixed number of categories when each system of teachings has an inconceivable number of major and minor empowerment texts? Briefly, all the methods of ripening in the unexcelled Secret Mantra are without a single exception included within the four categories of vase, secret, wisdom-knowledge, and word empowerments.

In addition, many scholars of the Sarma schools have raised numerous objections against certain empowerments found among the different vehicles, such as the empowerments of the shravakas and pratyekabuddhas found in the empowerment manuals of the Early Translation School of Secret Mantra.[8] Generally speaking, aside from the Secret Mantra, empowerments are not found in the sutras or in the Vinaya. Nevertheless, the context [of *The Great Assemblage]* demonstrates that all teachings are complete and included within the path of Mantrayana.[9] Practice of the short path of Mantrayana suffices for the sharpest type of person possessing the capacity for instantaneous realization, but people with gradual capacity are to be guided by means of the gradually ascending vehicles. The Two Segments describes this principle:

> At first, give the mending-purification,
> And then teach the Vaibhashika.
> Likewise, with the Sautrantika.

This describes the shravaka teachings. Next:

> After that, teach the Yogacharya.

This describes the Middle Way and so forth of the Mahayana vehicle.

> And next, teach the *Hevajra*.

This refers to the actual part of Vajrayana and corresponds to the prescribed gradual way of teaching.

Furthermore, regarding the context of taking precepts, most of the empowerment manuals state:

> The trainings of discipline—
> The precepts of individual liberation, of
>   bodhichitta,
> And the vidyadhara precepts of Mantrayana—
> I will always abide by and observe.

Even though empowerment manuals appear in various lengths, all agree on one single point: although the person who receives these precepts is indeed not eligible for the proper Vinaya title of *shramanera* or *bhikshu*, he still possesses the three complete sets of vows of Mantrayana. This can be understood simply by examining the previously mentioned steps of the Kalachakra empowerment. Again, one may think that the mandalas and empowerments of the different tantric vehicles should only be performed in accordance with their individual systems, and that it would be unreasonable to perform them exclusively in accordance with the Anuttara system. In fact, the lower vehicles and tantras are always included within the higher ones, but it is impossible for a higher vehicle or level of tantra to be included within the levels below. For example, the king is never controlled by the ministers; the ministers are always under the power of the king. Similarly, it is the nature of things that all the lower vehicles are completely contained within the Unexcelled Higher Vehicle. Nevertheless, the Sarma School empowerment text, *Vajra Garland*, teaches that the key point involving the different systems of bestowing empowerment is 'knowing one that frees all,' and does not divide them into different sections of tantra. It also explains the method used to divide the various sections of tantra, and how empowerment is conferred in accordance with each individual system.

The empowerments for the nine vehicles of the Nyingma school include two traditions:

- The method of conferring empowerment for all other mandalas in their totality within the Single Great Mandala of the Unexcelled; and
- The method of disclosing the mandalas of the individual sections of tantra, and then bestowing empowerment in accordance with each of their different systems.

In either case these empowerments are, without exception, part of the flawless tradition of Padmakara and the other sublime vidyadharas (awareness holders), panditas, and siddhas, and are exactly in accordance with the intent of the numerous tantras of the three yogas.[10] They are not fake teachings fabricated by dirty old family men of the Nyingma school dressed up as tantrikas. I merely mention this as an additional point.

Regarding why the empowerments are always divided into four types, you might ask, "What are the purpose and function of these four?" I will reply in terms of their basis of purification, the objects to be purified, the means of purifying, and the results of the purification.

All the aggregates and elements of beings—the 'vessel and its contents'—are the basis of purification of the vase empowerment. The speech and pranas present [within oneself] as syllables are the basis of purification of the secret empowerment. The essential elements and bindus present [within oneself] as great bliss are the basis of purification of the wisdom-knowledge empowerment. The mind essence that primordially is dharmakaya is the basis of purification of the word empowerment. Why is this? Because the basic materials are spontaneously present within oneself as these four aspects.

Then you may wonder, "Well, if they have been spontaneously present in myself since the beginning, what is the need for conferring the four empowerments?" The empowerments are necessary because of the existence of the following four deluded habitual tendencies which obscure the ground, seeds, or basic materials:

- The delusion of fixating on the world and beings as ordinary and solid,

- The delusion of fixating on the speech as ordinary,
- The delusion of fixating on the mind as ordinary, and
- The habitual tendencies of fixating on the three doors as being separate.

The means of purifying these four [fixations] is the four empowerments. Moreover, the purposes of the four empowerments are:

- To abandon the four types of desire that should be discarded: watching, laughing, touching, and embracing;
- To realize the four mudras that should be accomplished: the samaya mudra, the dharma mudra, the karma mudra, and the mahamudra;
- To savor the experiences of the four joys: the wisdom of joy, the wisdom of supreme joy, the wisdom of transcendent joy, and the wisdom of coemergent joy;
- To receive the four mandalas: the mandala of colored powder, the body mandala of the father and mother aspects, the mandala of the secret lotus, and the mandala of self-cognizant wakefulness;
- To authorize and make one suitable to perform the four practices: the development stage of the deity, the nadi-prana and the recitation, the swift path of the bindus, and the path of liberation of *Mahamudra* (The Great Seal) and *Dzogchen* (the Great Perfection);
- To comprehend the four views that should be realized: the views of Mind Only, the Middle Way, Secret Mantra, and Mahamudra and the Great Perfection;

- To accomplish the fruition of the four kayas: nirmanakaya, sambhogakaya, dharmakaya, and svabhavikakaya; and
- To gain mastery over the four activities for the welfare of others: pacifying, increasing, magnetizing and subjugating.

The purposes of and necessity for the four empowerments are included within these points. Their benefits are beyond the grasp of thought, as the *Secret Treasury of the Dakinis* mentions:

> When the unripened person has fully received
> the ripening empowerments and abides by the
> samayas,
> He will provisionally attain all siddhis, and
> ultimately achieve the fruition of the three
> kayas.

This is mentioned innumerable times in the various sections of the tantras.

The life-force of empowerment is embodied in the samayas. Therefore, in the context of the previously mentioned empowerments of the complete nine gradual vehicles, the detailed aspects of the samayas consist of the entire categories of precepts and trainings of both Sutra and Tantra.[11] Within the system of Mantrayana itself, the Sarma and Nyingma schools delineate the samayas individually.

In the Sarma system, as explained in the Kalachakra and other tantras, there is a fixed number of root downfalls for each of the Four Sections of Tantra.[12] Furthermore, the general system of Anuttara Tantra describes the twenty-one yogic disciplines, the samayas of the five families, the four root downfalls, the eight subsidiary downfalls and so forth.

The Nyingma system has twenty-seven root samayas, achieved by dividing each of the outer, inner, and secret samayas for body, speech, and mind into three. In addition, there are twenty-five subsidiary samayas, the twenty-one subtle samayas for the benefit of oneself, the forty-four samayas for the benefit of others, and so forth. In addition, there are the four great, natural samayas of the view—the samaya of nonexistence, the samaya of pervasiveness, the samaya of oneness, and the samaya of spontaneous presence—also called the 'special samayas' of the innermost Great Perfection.

In short, we should observe correctly and without violation all the samayas mentioned in all the commentaries on the tantras of the Nyingma and Sarma schools.

In particular, I shall now explicitly describe the samayas of meditation and post-meditation, eating, carrying, and observing for each of the four empowerments. Once you have received the vase empowerment, you should train in the development stage as the samaya of meditation. Do not let the three doors stray into delusion, and never separate from the notion of the deity in order to maintain the samaya of the post-meditation. Partake of the five meats and five nectars as the samaya of eating, and keep a qualified vajra and bell as the samaya of carrying. Finally, regard the world and beings as the mandala of deities and avoid wrong views as the samaya of observing. Be sure not to violate any of these.

Similarly, having received the secret empowerment, you should train in *tummo* as the samaya of meditation, and never forget the fire of the *atung* as the samaya of post-meditation. Partake of food and drink after consecrating them as wisdom nectar as the samaya of eating. Practice, without fail, prana-union twenty-one times daily as the samaya of carrying and avoid degenerating the element of bodhichitta as the samaya of observing.

Having obtained the empowerment of wisdom-knowledge, you should utilize an actual or mental consort as the samaya of meditation. Never separate from the experience of great bliss as the samaya of post-meditation. Enjoy the manner of union as the samaya of eating and treasure the *kunda* bodhichitta as the samaya of carrying. Give up wrong views about females, who have the nature of knowledge, as the samaya of observing.

The samaya of the meditation for the precious word empowerment of indivisible great bliss is to train in the nature of unity beyond concepts. The samaya of the post-meditation is to avoid straying into complete delusion, and instead be inseparable from the experience of union. The samaya of eating is to let dharmata enjoy dharmata. The samaya of carrying is never to depart from the key points of the view, meditation, and action. The samaya of observing is to remain unspoiled by accepting or rejecting, clinging or fixating, on anything that takes place.

If you keep these samayas for practicing the four empowerments, not violating them for a single moment, all the qualities of Secret Mantra in their entirety will manifest within your being like an overflowing heap. You will quickly realize the fruition of the four kayas. All the temporary and ultimate qualities will appear effortlessly as the spontaneous Great Perfection. So, it is said.

To present these merely indicative general explanations of the four empowerments to the venerable ears of someone like yourself, who has gained mastery over the treasury of the dharma, is the same as trying to teach the six syllable [mantra] to Avalokiteshvara.[13] Moreover, learned and accomplished masters of other dharma traditions would certainly ignore these silly, pointless scribblings written by my ignorant self. Indeed, I'm only putting my pen to hard work. Nevertheless, when I wrote this down, I thought, "Wouldn't it be nice if my efforts would create the right circumstance for awakening all the supposed dharma practitioners from their ignorant slumber, especially those so-called monks and followers who, although they pretend to have entered the path of Secret Mantra, haven't taken to heart even a single verse relating how to practice Vajrayana?"

THE DIVIDING LINE

Now, returning to your question about the dividing line between truly obtaining or not obtaining empowerment, and to your additional detailed inquiry about people who practice the third empowerment in name only while merely becoming an embarrassment to the Buddhadharma: I shall present my understanding in the following concise points.

Someone who wishes to enter the gate of the precious Buddhadharma in general, and the vajra vehicle of Secret Mantra in particular, and who possesses the attitude of renunciation and the sincere desire to attain enlightenment, should connect with a qualified spiritual master. The master should not be a charlatan guru or a demonic imposter. The student should have devotion free from hypocrisy, and faith that resolves the master to be a buddha in person. With a noble heart free from desiring material gain or veneration, the master himself should accept the disciple and guide him on the path in accordance with his degree of mental capacity. When the disciple has become a suitable recipient and at the appropriate time, the master should confer the vase empowerment within a mandala through either the extensive or concise ritual procedures.

Here, the main point is to confer the vase empowerment and give its pointing-out instruction while focusing on a method that successfully reduces the disciple's habitual tendencies and deluded clinging to an outer and inner, gross and subtle, solid and ordinary world with beings. Free from platitudes and mere lip-service and exactly in accordance with the master's words, the disciple should understand how the world and beings, everything animate or inanimate and comprised of the aggregates, elements and sense factors, has, since the very outset, never been anything but the mandala of the deity. Right then, through the master's kindness and instructions, the disciple's obscuration of momentary delusion is cleared away. He is able to understand how the external world is in fact a celestial palace and its inhabitants are indeed a mandala of deities.

In particular, through the conferring of the five knowledge empowerments, the disciple understands and realizes exactly 'how it really is.' He realizes that our inherent possession, the five aggregates, are primordially the five male buddhas, the five elements are primordially the five female buddhas, the five poisons are primordially the five wisdoms, and so forth. This signifies having obtained the vase empowerment and having embodied its objective.

In fact, it is necessary to purify our karmic perception of everything outer and inner, the world and beings, as being ordinary and solid. Consider the methods and auspicious coincidences necessary for this to occur. During any empowerment ritual, at the time of the descent of the wisdom beings, a blindfold is tied on the recipient in order to interrupt the thoughts that cling to visible forms as ordinary. Music is played to stop the thoughts that cling to sound as ordinary. Smoke prepared from substances such as incense and resin, causing the wisdom to descend, is spread to halt the thoughts of smell as ordinary. Consecrated nectar is given to interrupt thoughts that fixate on taste as ordinary. The physical position of the sevenfold posture of Vairochana or the vajra posture is taken to stop thoughts that cling to touch as ordinary. Finally, the steps of visualization, emanating, and absorbing are taken to interrupt the deluded clinging to our mind as ordinary.

Moreover, the master, by the power of making the blessings descend through his own steadfast samadhi, interrupts for a short while the disciple's deluded perception of ordinary body, speech, and mind. The foremost disciple experiences the unobscured dawning of self-existing, coemergent wakefulness. The next best [disciple] experiences pure perception with overwhelming and intense devotion as the manifestation of experience blazes forth, while the disciple of lesser caliber should at least feel slightly exhilarated.

The combination of these different meditative visualizations and skillful means evokes the wisdom that is the nature of empowerment within the disciple's mind. The seal of the empowerment is given to point out what has been brought forth, to stabilize it, and to assure it will never depart from this nature.

If the nature of the empowerment has arisen in the disciple's mind, then he has received the real empowerment, regardless of whether the superficial articles of empowerment are placed on his head. Moreover, should he realize the nature of the vase empowerment with regards to the path of liberation, during the development stage practices he need not depend upon a mind-made practice of imaginary imputations, for he is liberated from the 'good clinging' of fixating on shapes and colors as the deity. For such a person all that appears and exists dawns as all-encompassing purity, and therefore all attachment and aggression towards self and other, enemy and friend, good and evil, and so forth are naturally liberated.

As long as the nature of the empowerment is not understood, even if a mandala were arranged to fill the entire country, and hundreds of thousands of vases and so forth were placed upon the disciple's head, and he were given as much water from the vases as he could carry off, his mind would remain unmoved from its former ordinary state, without any impairment whatsoever, to its mundane deluded clinging.

When the nature of even the vase empowerment has not arisen within the disciple's mind, he is not eligible to receive the higher empowerments, and will in any case not comprehend them. When the seeds of the ripening empowerments have not been sown, how can the leaves and fruit of the liberating path grow forth? Further empowerments will therefore be nothing more than futile effort on the part of both master and disciple, and, in the worst case, will form the circumstances for the downfall and violation of divulging the secrecy of Mantrayana.

On the contrary, when the auspicious coincidence of master and disciple—nectar and suitable vessel—come together, the vase empowerment does ripen the body of the disciple so that his aggregates, nadis, and elements are purified and the five poisons dawn as wisdom. Through the power of that, he then becomes a suitable recipient for the secret empowerment.

Such a disciple can, by means of the physical mandala of master and consort, be given the secret substance on his tongue and have the nature of the empowerment pointed out. Thereby, his deluded clinging to ordinary speech is purified and he realizes that the Vajra Speech has been spontaneously present since the beginning. At this point, he recognizes whatever is heard as the continuity of mantra and gains mastery over recitation and utterance, emanating and absorbing, and over any type of vajra recitation, silent recitation, and so forth. By training in the blazing and dripping of tummo, melting and refining the bindu, as well as the descent, retention, reversal, and spreading [of bodhichitta], accomplishment is attained, and the disciple becomes a suitable recipient for the wisdom-knowledge empowerment.

Such a person can, by means of an actual or mental mudra, be led into a direct manifestation and experience of the four joys whereby the coemergent wisdom of bliss and emptiness is pointed out. As indicated thereby, the disciple realizes all other mental thought formations—such as joy or sorrow, hot or cold, roughness or smoothness, pleasure or displeasure, desire or anger, and so forth—to be coemergent wisdom.

When the nature of the third empowerment has genuinely arisen in the disciple's mind, and he perceives how his mind in actuality is the essence of the Vajra Mind, he has become a suitable recipient for the word empowerment. This king of all empowerments, the empowerment of great bliss or the precious word empowerment, is in all the Great Perfection teachings called 'the empowerment of the expression of awareness.' When this is correctly pointed out, the disciple can recognize, decide, and finally resolve that all phenomena of samsara and nirvana are the vajra wisdom of the indivisible four kayas, the great all-pervasive innate self-awareness that is unfabricated and spontaneously present. Thus, he directly and easily realizes the meaning of how the ground, path, and fruition, and how the view, meditation, and action—in short, how the naked vital point of all the 84,000 doors to the dharma—are totally embodied within present ordinary wakefulness. Having realized this, the disciple transcends the domain of hope and fear, dualistic fixation, accepting and rejecting, and captures the stronghold in which whatever occurs is the play of original wakefulness.

This correct procedure for bestowing and receiving the four empowerments is indispensable, since all the Great Perfection teachings of the Nyingma school outline a definite system for conferring and practicing the essential meaning of these four empowerments [in sequential order], with an interval of months or years between each. The disciple becomes a siddha upon completion of the four empowerments.

However, nowadays[14] many followers of the Sarma and Nyingma schools trade the teachings of Secret Mantra for food and material gain. Although the important key points of development and completion, ripening and liberation, did indeed fall upon their ears, they lack personal experience. They consider it sufficient merely to have learned the terminology of the tantric root texts and the elaborate details of the ritual procedures. At the same time, they compete in superficial matters such as the melodiousness of voice and ritual instruments, and go to the houses of benefactors offering the promise of highest gain. There they pass the time pursuing offerings and consuming food and drink, primarily wine and meat slaughtered for their sake.

Even people like myself, so-called 'lamas' who have not even taken to heart the correct meaning of taking refuge, sneak about like mice, feigning the virtuous appearance and conduct respected by common people. While in our hearts we aim at nothing other than material goods and income, we expound the dharma, confer empowerments, give instructions, ordain monks and nuns, perform consecrations and undertake rituals for the sake of the dead. Motivated by presumption, we shy away from nothing, though we lack the power to act in the capacity of a vajra master. The insignificant amount of food and material wealth gained as a result of this activity leaves a trail of nonvirtue. Spending our lives in this way, we wreak disaster upon ourselves, our followers, and whoever is linked with us. Many so-called 'lamas,' lacking even the virtue and power of having chanted as much as one rosary of the six syllable [mantra], find it enough to know merely how to hold a vajra and bell, because they are an incarnation of such-and-such sublime personage or belong to a special bloodline. They proclaim that whoever connects with them will be benefited, yet their behavior is akin to the example of showing a deer's tail in order to pass off donkey meat as venison, or tying a bell on the neck of a cow that doesn't give milk in order to sell it.

On the other hand, the arhats, panditas, and siddhas

of India gladdened householders and common people by teaching the law of karma, the bases of purity—love, compassion, joy, and impartiality—the progressive and reverse order of dependent origination,[15] and the merit of generosity. Moreover, not a single source mentions the bestowal of empowerments in the way that we Tibetans perform them.

Nowadays in [17th-century] Tibet, Kham, Kongpo, and other districts, certain lamas make concerted efforts to collect offerings and hoard food and wealth by trading empowerments and teachings as commodities, under the pretense of inspiring people to virtue and benefiting sentient beings. Crowds of people, many of whom do not even know the alphabet and just happen to be around, are gathered for the empowerments by deceitful means such as beating drums, blowing conches, performing dances and plays, arranging group practices for young maidens, and giving communal meals.

Many of these people, never questioning whether or not they are a suitable recipient nor thinking about the wisdom that is the nature of the empowerment, participate in empowerments half-heartedly, aiming merely to entertain themselves and enjoy some companionship. Others who feign faith or understanding of the dharma may participate in empowerments for the sake of dispelling sickness or evil influences, reducing the effect of their inauspicious year,[16] or to remedy an ominous divination or astrological horoscope.

In such cases, regardless of whether or not the lama explains the empowerment, the participants are completely obscured by the 'three defects of the vessel' and the 'six impurities,'[17] and will not understand the meaning. Believing that empowerment is a mere touch on the head with ritual articles, they walk away from the ceremony with vacant gazes, lacking the faintest idea about what the master pointed out. This type of empowerment ceremony is indeed quite common.

Some people claim that empowerments given to a crowd of laypeople are not the complete four empowerments of Secret Mantra, and that no fault exists since these are just permission-blessings, or entrustments.[18] But actually, even an entrustment involves the samaya commitment to keep the deity in mind and to do the practices of 'approach and accomplishment' and so forth. During such a ceremony one has to repeat the taking of the precepts of refuge, bodhichitta, and the samayas of the five families, and since most ordinary people cannot possibly know the principles of what should be adopted and avoided, both myself and others are therefore indeed at fault for being involved in such affairs.[19] Incidentally, as it has been taught in the sutras that people who live off selling the sacred dharma are reborn in a hell where they eat flaming iron balls and drink molten lead, it seems as though the dharma practitioners of the present age have incredibly great courage.

Another aspect: the followers of the New Schools hold that the above-mentioned link between master and disciple depends upon ritualistic procedure. When they confer an empowerment, they maintain that all the ritualistic procedures, such as the liturgical arrangement [for the empowerment] and so forth, must follow the explanations of the authoritative scriptures, and therefore, they place exclusive emphasis on these procedures such as the self-initiation, etc.[20] The adherents of the Nyingma School advocate that blessings depend on the mantra, and therefore place great emphasis on the recitation.

In my own ignorant opinion, all of these must come together as a foundation. In particular, it is my understanding that the vital point is to receive the blessings and realize the nature of the empowerment that is pointed out, which is based on the strength of the meeting between the master's blessings and the disciple's devotion. It appears to me that once you receive such a blessing, [realization of the nature of the empowerment] does not depend solely upon a material empowerment being or not being conferred.

For instance, due to the power of Tilopa displaying a cotton rag scorched by sparks and twelve other symbols, Naropa realized the nature of the four empowerments. The dakini Secret Wisdom (*Guhya Jnana, Sangwa Yeshe*) was also known as Sun and Moon Attainment (*Nyida Ngödrub*), as Sukhasiddhi when she transmitted the Cutting Practice, and as the dakini Leykyi Wangmo in the Nyingma School. When she conferred empowerment upon Guru Padmasambhava, she transformed him into the letter HUNG. Swallowing the HUNG, she sent it through her body and emitted it through her secret lotus, whereby Padmasambhava received the complete four empowerments and attained the supreme accomplishment of Mahamudra.

When Padmasambhava was about to leave Tibet for the Southwestern Continent, he bestowed the profound teaching of *Padma Nyingtig* upon King Lhasey and four other disciples on Mount Hepori at Samye. In a single moment, he transformed that very place into the realm of Sukhavati and brought them to maturity by emanating and absorbing rays of light.

Moreover, when Lord Maitripa finally met the great master Shavaripa after seeking him with disregard to his own body and life, his being was ripened and liberated simply by Shavaripa placing a hand upon his head.

The siddha Khyungpo Naljor realized the nature of empowerment when the dakini Niguma poured a skull cup full of secret water for him and pointed a finger at his heart.[21]

The siddha Orgyenpa realized the nature of empowerment when a yogini in the form of a courtesan gave him a bowl of soup.

There is also the story that the terton Guru Chöwang placed a piece of excrement on the top of the head of the Nepalese man Bharo Vihardhara and poured urine into his mouth. Through this, Bharo remained in undefiled coemergent wisdom for seven days and was liberated.[22]

The learned and accomplished Kyoshey Tönpa expelled Machik Labdrön from the empowerment assembly, beat her and threw her into the river, through which she realized the wisdom of the empowerment and could traverse freely through walls.

Dampa Gommön, who transmitted the Pacifying Practice, gave Chupa Dartsön a cup of tea and a large bag of *tsampa*, saying "This is a substitute for the empowerment ritual," whereby Chupa Dartsön received the blessings and attained realization equal to that of his master.

Countless such stories abound. Obviously, the vital point of empowerment is to receive the blessings so that original wakefulness dawns in our being. Therefore, there is no point in listing the details of whether or not the qualifications of the place, master, and disciple are complete as taught in the tantras, or whether there must be a fixed number of disciples and so forth. In these times, when questions regarding the nature of the empowerment, the way to implement it in practical experience, and the points of the samaya commitments, etc. are left behind on the pages of books, and masters as well as disciples do as they please and what feels most enjoyable, these discussions between the two of us will cause nothing more than annoyance in the hearts of others.

In any case, regarding the purpose: once you receive the vase empowerment, your aggregates and elements are ripened into deities; and when you correctly understand the symbols and meaning of the development stage and put them into practice, the seed of nirmanakaya is sown.

When you obtain the secret empowerment; understand that the inhalation, abidance, and exhalation of the breath is mantra; and implement this in practice; you will be implanted with the seed of sambhogakaya.

Having received the knowledge empowerment, when mental occurrences and thought formations arise as dharmata and you sustain coemergent wisdom, you have sown the seed of dharmakaya.

By obtaining the word empowerment and resolving that samsara and nirvana are equal, and by sustaining the practice like the flow of a river without straying from the state of unity beyond concepts, you accomplish the undivided state of the essence body, svabhavikakaya, at best within this lifetime, or next best in the bardo. After this, by emanations generated by aspirations and compassion, you perfect the welfare of beings as a great, effortless and spontaneous accomplishment.

Sowing the Seeds *

Padmasambhava, Chokgyur Lingpa,
and Jamgön Kongtrül Lodrö Thaye

This has two points: a brief statement mentioning the topic,
and the detailed explanation of the meaning.

A BRIEF STATEMENT MENTIONING THE TOPIC

The *Lamrim Yeshe Nyingpo* root text says:

Now, for the steps of planting the seeds:º

Having already trained your being through the general
paths, then enter the stages of the special paths. The first
of these is the steps for planting the seeds of buddhahood
within yourself.[23]

THE DETAILED EXPLANATION OF THE MEANING

This has two parts: The actual planting of the seeds, and
explaining their life-force, the samayas.

THE ACTUAL PLANTING OF THE SEEDS

This has three points: The person to whom empowerment is
to be given, the empowerments to be conferred, and the way
of conferring empowerment.

---

*Extracted from Lamrim Yeshe Nyingpo and *The Light of Wisdom*.

THE PERSON TO WHOM EMPOWERMENT
IS TO BE GIVEN

The *Lamrim Yeshe Nyingpo* root text says:

> Having motivated his being through renunciation,
>   the person of Mahayana nature:
> Should train his mind thoroughly in the twofold
>   bodhichitta. :
> Within this person of good fortune, who wishes
>   swiftly to attain buddhahood ...

The person to whom empowerment is to be given is described in the *Ornament*:

> Who through knowledge doesn't dwell in
>   existence,
> And through compassion doesn't dwell in peace.

In this way, such a person should possess the Mahayana potential and his being should be motivated by true renunciation—through knowledge and compassion—of the two extremes of samsaric existence and nirvanic peace. The signs of that are mentioned in the *Ornament of the Sutras:*

> To precede an action with compassion,
> To have aspiration and patience,
> And to correctly engage in virtue:
> These are taught as the signs of the [Mahayana]
>   potential.

Such a person should have awakened this nature by means of learning and so forth. Through having trained his mind fully in the twofold precious bodhichitta, conventional and ultimate, he should desire to quickly realize and achieve the state of buddhahood for the benefit of sentient beings, in as short a time as one life, without requiring the long duration or hardship of three incalculable aeons.[24] Such a person of excellent fortune is a suitable vessel for planting the ripening seeds.

THE EMPOWERMENTS TO BE CONFERRED

This has two parts: Brief statement, and detailed explanation.

BRIEF STATEMENT

The *Lamrim Yeshe Nyingpo* root text says:

> Since his being abides as the nature of the four vajras⦂
> Of body, speech, mind, and wisdom, ⦂
> Plant the seeds of the four empowerments⦂
> Through the skillful means of the Unexcelled Secret Mantra.⦂

The *King of Empowerment Tantra* says:

> If you didn't possess the supreme power yourself,
> How could you obtain it by being empowered?
> Even if you empower peas or buckwheat to be rice,
> They will never produce real rice.

Similarly, the nature of the four kayas, as the concurrent causes that are primordially present within the mind-stream

45

of each sentient being, become actualized by the methods of Mantra as the co-operating conditions. That is to say, even though the nadi constituents as the vajra body, the speech pranas as the vajra speech, the bindus as the vajra mind, and the all-ground as the vajra wisdom, are spontaneously perfected from the very beginning as the natures of the four vajras, their capabilities are not manifest as they lie dormant within the cocoon of temporary defilements. It is by means of the extraordinarily skillful rituals that are the intent of the Unexcelled Tantras —the ultimate pinnacle of the vajra vehicles, which has neither been proclaimed in the Paramita teachings nor in any of the lower tantras of Secret Mantra— that the seeds for ripening [these four vajras] into the four kayas should be planted in the [disciple's] mind-stream by means of being initiated into the four mandalas of support and then being conferred the four empowerments of the vase and so forth.

DETAILED EXPLANATION

The *Lamrim Yeshe Nyingpo* root text says:

> The vase empowerment that purifies the body and
>   the nadis⸱
> Is the seed of the vajra body and nirmanakaya.⸱
> The secret empowerment that purifies the speech
>   and the pranas⸱
> Is the seed of the vajra speech and sambhogakaya.⸱
> The phonya empowerment that purifies the mind
>   and the bindus⸱
> Is the seed of the vajra mind and dharmakaya.⸱

The ultimate empowerment that purifies the
    habitual tendencies of the all-ground§
Is the seed of the vajra wisdom and
    svabhavikakaya.§

How should the seeds of the four empowerments be
planted in the worthy person? The *Talgyur Root Tantra* says:

In order to perfectly purify
A sentient being's four factors of body, speech,
    mind, and cognition,[25]
A worthy person should be ripened
By means of the four empowerments.

According to this statement, the system of Unexcelled
Yoga, *Anuttara Yoga*, has the definite number of four empowerments because of the relationship between ground,
path, and fruition. Their basis is exclusively the vajra body
endowed with the six elements and all the nadis, pranas, and
bindus.[26] In terms of this basis for those who are to be reborn
in the higher realms, the eyes and the nadi-knot of the navel
center are formed at the early stages in the womb. Following
that, the five chakras are gradually formed until the 72,000
nadis and the [complete] body are produced. These 'consti-
tuting nadis are, therefore, the main objects of purification
connected with the body. Since the body is also the basis for
the speech and mind, as well as being the coarsest object of
purification, it is the first to be purified.

In order to do that, the elaborate vase empowerment is
conferred. This consists of the benefiting and enabling aspects, within any of the three supreme image mandalas. The
vase empowerment purifies the waking state and the defilements of body and the nadis, brings an end to the thoughts

that fixate on the five aggregates, and defeats the Mara of the Aggregates.[27] It empowers you to practice the yoga of form, the development stage of regarding the aggregates, elements, and sense-sources as the mandala of the three seats of completeness.[28] It also plants the seed for temporarily attaining a status equal to the eighth bhumi of the causal [vehicles], and for ultimately realizing the fruition of the vajra body, the nirmanakaya that is the unity of appearance and emptiness.[29]

Based on the primary and subsidiary pranas within these nadis, confused thoughts are produced inwardly and various voice expressions occur outwardly. These 'moving pranas' are, therefore, the main objects of purification connected with speech. Because speech is more subtle than body, the speech and pranas are purified after the vase empowerment.

In order to do so, the foundation used is the 'thatness of self' of the body mandala, which is connected with the three profound empowerments.[30] Conferring the secret empowerment of the special 'thatness of mantra syllable' within the mandala of the *bhaga* — based on the white and red bodhichitta, which are not to be shown to the unworthy — purifies the dream state, the defilements of speech and pranas, brings the thoughts that cling to form as a deity to an end,[31] and defeats the Mara of Conflicting Emotions. It empowers you to practice the path of completion stage with attributes, the self-consecration of recognizing prana as indivisible from mantra. It also plants the seeds for attaining a status equal to the causal ninth bhumi, and for realizing the fruition of vajra speech, the sambhogakaya that is the unity of luminosity and emptiness.

The essences of the elements, the bodhichitta bindus, are supported by the nadis and pranas. These white and red elements move back and forth like the flow of water within the nadis, which are like irrigation channels, and by means of the moving force of the pranas. This causes the production of the mind's experience of a perceiver and something perceived. These 'arrayed bindus' are, therefore, the objects of purification connected with mind. Since mind is more subtle than speech, the mind and the bindus are purified after the secret empowerment.

In order to do so, the conferring of the empowerment that indicates the 'wisdom of example by means of the knowledge-maiden within the mandala of relative bodhichitta, the 'thatness of deity,' purifies the state of deep sleep, and the defilements of mind and bindus, brings the eighty innate thought states to an end, and defeats the Mara of the Lord of Death.[32] It empowers you to practice the path of the mandala-circle for accomplishing the wisdom of example through the three types of mudra.[33] It also plants the seeds for attaining a status equal to the causal tenth bhumi and for realizing the fruition of vajra mind, the dharmakaya that is the unity of bliss and emptiness.

All these nadis, pranas, and bindus are, however, nothing other than manifestations of clinging to a perceiver and something perceived, due to the 'forming mind' having stirred from the all-ground for manifold tendencies.[34] This all-ground is, therefore, the chief of all objects of purification.

In order to purify the all-ground, along with the habitual tendencies for ignorance, which is exceedingly more subtle than all the former factors, the empowerment of the word and symbol is conferred. This indicates sublime self-knowing within the mandala of ultimate bodhichitta, the 'thatness of wisdom,' and purifies the state of union, the 'elaboration of seeping bliss,' as well as the obscuration of transition of the combined three doors along with its habitual tendencies. It brings the dualistic thoughts of occurring sensation to an end, and defeats the Mara of the Divine Son.[35] It empowers you to practice the universal wisdom of Dzogchen, the paths of primordial purity and spontaneous presence. It also plants the seed or potential within your stream-of-being for attaining a status equal to the causal eleventh bhumi and for realizing the fruition of vajra wisdom, the svabhavikakaya that is the unity of awareness and emptiness.

THE WAY OF CONFERRING EMPOWERMENT

The *Lamrim Yeshe Nyingpo* root text says:

> All these are given to the ordinary person.§
> Along with preparations, they are initiated and
>   ripened.§
> Some people of sharp faculties are introduced by
>   means of symbols.§
> The others, the supreme ones, are liberated merely
>   by samadhi.§

By means of which procedures are these four empowerments to be conferred? All empowerments have many extraordinary ways of being conferred, depending on the different masters who confer them and the different capacities of disciples upon whom they are being conferred. In terms of the common person, the procedures are comprised of the following three: subject, object, and action.

The subject, the vajra master, should have gained mastery in the five aspects of Mantra: the thatness of deity, of self, of *guhya-mantra*, of recitation, and of emanation and absorption.[36] The actions to be performed, similar to a vessel being cleaned before pouring a precious liquid, are the preparations of deity, vase, and disciple, preceded by the ritual for the land.[37]

Having propitiated and offered homage to the mandala of lines, colored powder, or arranged decorations, [the vajra master] initiates himself or throws the flower of awareness and receives permission.[38] Following that, he initiates [the disciple] into the outer mandala of attributes and the inner mandala of wisdom.[39]

Upon the disciple whose stream-of-being has thus been purified, the subject [the master] then confers empowerment by means of the special ritual of combined substance, mantra, and samadhi.[40] Through this, the gross and subtle three doors of the object, the disciple, are pointed out to be primordially pure, as the deities of the 'three seats of completeness.' This either clears away or reduces the particular defilements to be purified, and revives intrinsic wakefulness, the object of attainment, to a sufficient degree.[41]

In this way, to be empowered means this special quality of [being infused with] the cause for either realizing the wisdoms of the two stages of the path in actuality, or, being ripened so as to have the capacity for this realization to definitely arise, just as a seed will ripen when planted where water, manure, warmth and moisture are assembled. The *Heruka Assemblage* describes this:

> It is called empowerment because the one upon
> whom it is conferred
> Has his stream-of-being purified and obtains the
> power.

Some extraordinary people of naturally sharp faculties who possess the residual karma of former training can, without having to depend upon elaborate steps of rituals, receive in completeness the four empowerments that ripen their stream-of-being. This is achieved by means of simply a symbolic gesture and having the meaning pointed out. For example, the *Vidyadhara Assemblage Root Tantra* says:

> When a master endowed with all the
>   qualifications
> Confers the empowerment of blessings
> By means of some substance such as a torma,
> Colored sand, a mirror, or a vase,
> One obtains the supreme essence of all mandalas,
> The four empowerments, the thatness of the
>   fourth.

This statement refers to the countless number of profound empowerments such as the four circular empowerments of the master, and so forth, given by the followers of the Early Translation School of Secret Mantra, or the progressive stages of consecration of Vajra Yogini given by the followers of the Later Translation Schools.[42]

Some other people, gifted to the highest degree, have their stream-of-being ripened and liberated simply through the power of the samadhi and blessings of a qualified master. When the coincidence of vessel and contents has come about, original wakefulness dawns directly. This, being the empowerment of vajra wisdom, is the king of all empowerments. Examples of this can be found in the life stories of many of the accomplished masters of the Noble Land as well as of the past accomplished lineage masters of Tibet.

Mentioning the additional topics briefly, there are six points: 1) the identity of empowerment, 2) the definition, 3) the divisions, 4) the way of conferring, 5) the defects of not receiving, 6) and the benefits of having received empowerment.

1) THE IDENTITY OF EMPOWERMENT

Empowerment is that which ripens one to realize intrinsic wakefulness, the object of attainment, or which ripens one to have the definite potential for this realization to occur.[43]

2) THE DEFINITION

The word *abhishincha* means 'fully sprinkling' or 'anointing.'[44] The word 'empowerment' is therefore used since the defilements to be purified are sprinkled or washed away, and since the special capacity for being suitable to cultivate the path and attain the fruition is established. The *Hevajra Tantra* says:

> Because of sprinkling and anointing,
> It is therefore called empowerment.

3) THE DIVISIONS

Among the three types of empowerments of ground, path and fruition, the empowerment at the time of the ground must initially be received from a master. This is because a particular means of ripening should be received before studying or meditating upon the paths of Mantra.

The empowerment at the time of the path can later be received from either the master or yourself, being someone endowed with the precepts. This is because it is an empowerment to further develop the continuum of the earlier empowerments with which your being has been ripened.

The empowerment at the time of fruition is conferred at the moment of the end of the stream, when you have perfected the path of learning, because it is the empowerment that unites you with the ultimate fruition.[45]

4) THE WAY OF CONFERRING

As Drilbupa stated, conferring empowerment must be preceded by a mandala:

> The Vajradhara has taught
> That conferring empowerment is preceded by a
> mandala.

There are three types of mandala: the natural wisdom mandala, the mandala of superior samadhi or emanation, and the experience mandala of awareness. Respectively, these mandalas are the domains of noble beings, masters who are a perfect buddha, or someone abiding on the paths of consummation, seeing, or cultivation.

According to the different types of disciples, the masters who have attained the 'matching stability' in samadhi confer through the medium of a mere support for visualization. They use colored sand to initiate those less gifted, painted cloth for those of medium ability, and heaps [of grain] for the more gifted ones. It is also taught that a master confers empowerment through the medium of his own body to the very intelligent among the most gifted disciples.

Concerning the empowerments which are to be conferred within these mandalas, in general, all the Anuttara

Yoga empowerments at the time of the ground definitely consist of four [empowerments]. This is because there are four defilements to be purified, four paths of development and completion which purify them, and four kayas as the result of being purified. The *Subsequent Essence Tantra* therefore explains:

> The [empowerments of] the master, the secret,
>   and the knowledge,
> And immediately thereafter, the fourth;
> Thus, to purify the defilements of conceptual
>   thinking
> There are four types of empowerment.

The *Compendium,* in agreement with all the tantras of the Old and New Schools, further states:

> The vase empowerment is the first,
> The second is the secret empowerment.
> The third is that of wisdom-knowledge,
> And likewise, there is the fourth.

In particular, our own system of the Early Translations has the divisions of tantra, statement, and instruction: [46]

The Magical Net Tantra [47] teaches to confer the outer ten benefiting empowerments[48] upon the devoted disciple; then to confer the inner five enabling empowerments[49] upon the industrious one capable of benefiting himself, others, and both; and finally, to confer the secret three profound empowerments upon the type who possesses the yogic discipline of having equalized conduct and insight.[50]

The Embodiment Scripture of Statement [of Anu Yoga] teaches to confer, within the *Scripture* root mandala, the thirty-six empowerments of the complete four rivers, according to the stated topics of Tantra, upon the special disciple who is inclined to the profound meaning and is a naturally worthy recipient. Also, it teaches to confer upon the common disciple who is inclined to the extensive, and is a worthy recipient due to training, the thirty-six root empowerments divided into 831 complex branch empowerments after having divided up the complete *Scripture* mandala together with its subsidiary aspects.[51]

The two systems of Tantra and Instruction can again be condensed into four empowerments: the outer, the inner, the sadhana, and the secret.[52]

The Instruction Ati Yoga emphasizes the empowerment of awareness display and has individual ways of conferring it, according to the systems of the Three Sections of Dzogchen.

According to the Instruction Section, the elaborate empowerment purifies the defilements of the three doors and of delusion concerning objects of knowledge. The unelaborate empowerment induces the capacity of Body, Speech, and Mind and of self-existing luminosity. The very unelaborate empowerment introduces the mind-essence as being free from basis and root and empowers one to practice the wisdom of primordial purity. The extremely unelaborate empowerment empowers one to practice the directness of spontaneously present luminosity.

According to the Sadhana Section,[53] the *Sacred Embodiment of Sugatas* generally teaches four types: The disciple with anger should have the outer empowerment conferred by means of the 108 outer and inner substances, such as the vase, in order to take liberation as the path. The disciple with pride have the inner empowerment conferred by means of the body in order to take the deity as the path. The disciple with desire should have the secret empowerment conferred by means of the consort in order to take union as the path. The disciple with ignorance should have the empowerment of thatness conferred by means of the mind in order to take conceptual thinking as the path.

5) THE DEFECTS OF NOT RECEIVING EMPOWERMENT

The *Buddhakapala Tantra* says:[54]

> For example, a lute with all the workmanship
> completed
> Cannot be played if it lacks the cords.
> Similarly, lacking empowerment,
> One will not accomplish the mantra and
> meditation.

6) THE BENEFIT OF HAVING RECEIVED EMPOWERMENT

Numberless quotations express these benefits, including the *Awesome Lightning:*[55]

> Perform the deeds of initiating
> Into the mandala of the supreme secret,
> Of receiving the siddhis and of conferring
> empowerment.
> Through that, within even this very life,
> You will attain the state of buddhahood,
> Not to mention the other siddhis.

The Destroyer of All Evil Deeds and Obscurations

This is the general procedure of empowerments for
accepting the devoted ones,
according to *The Pure Gold Great Perfection,
the Heart Essence of Samantabhadra*

Padmasambhava and Chokgyur Lingpa

HOMAGE TO GURU SAMANTABHADRA!

*In order to accept the devoted ones, the general procedure of
empowerment is taught.*

*As to the preparatory, main, and concluding rituals, first
carefully arrange the mandala and lay out the vase with articles, and essences.*

*The representations of Body, Speech, and Mind and the of-
fering materials should be gathered without any lacking.*

Then, perform a full empowerment recitation.

*The vajra master should enter into samadhi
And relieve the disciples of hindrances and mishap.*

*Having bathed, and wearing clean clothing, prostrate, offer
a gift, and respectfully say:*

> HO
> Guru, glorious Vajrasattva,
> Please regard me with loving kindness.
> Lead us out of the place of samsara
> And let us enter the citadel of liberation.

Supplicate like that, then take refuge, arouse bodhicitta, and say༔:

HO༔
Sugatas, peaceful and wrathful victorious ones,༔
   please consider me.༔
From today and until the essence of
   enlightenment,༔
I will not abandon the samayas of body, speech
   and mind, even at the cost of my life.༔

Consecrate the samaya water with OM AH HUM༔

HO༔
In the continuity of Body, Speech, and Mind,༔
By this, you will accomplish all the siddhis.༔
If you do not guard it, you will be born in the
   hells.༔
Therefore, keep the samayas.༔

OM AH HUM VAJRA KA VA CI SAMAYA RAKSHA TISHTHA

Take the oath one-pointedly, and say:
SAMAYA IDAN NARAKAN༔

Above the head, in the throat, in the heart-center,
   in the navel,༔
In the secret place, and in the soles of the feet,༔
Are A, SU, NRI, TRI, PRE, and DU.༔
Upon these the actual forms of the Body, Speech
   and Mind of the victorious ones,༔
The syllables RAM YAM and KHAM blaze down.༔
   Imagine that the surging forth of wisdom fire,
   wind, and water༔

Burns, scatters, and washes, after which they are
purified.°

RAM SPHARANA PHAT. YAM SPHARANA PHAT. KHAM
SPHARANA PHAT°

OM DAHA DAHA SARVA NARAKA GATE HETUM HUM
PHAT°

OM PACA PACA SARVA PRETAKA GATE HETUM HUM
PHAT°

OM MATHA MATHA SARVA TIRYAKA GATE HETUM
HUM PHAT°

OM CACHINDHA CACHINDHA SARVA NRI GATE
HETUM HUM PHAT°

OM TRATA TRATA SARVA ASURA GATE HETUM HUM
PHAT°

OM PHRITA PHRITA SARVA SURA GATE HETUM HUM
PHAT°

Also visualize the body to be a mass of light.°

From the state of emptiness, upon a lotus and
moon,°
Is the white Bhagavan Vajrasattva,°
Holding vajra and bell, seated in half-vajra
posture,° Visualized as ornamented with silks
and jewels.°
The three places are marked with OM AH and
HUM.° The inconceivable wisdom gatherings°
Of Body, Speech, and Mind of all the assemblies
of mandala deities are emanated and absorbed.°

OM AH HUM JNANA KAYA VAKA CITTA ABESHAYA A AH°

Dissolving again and again, play the musical instruments. When the signs of the descent of great blessings occur, stabilize the wisdom with:

OM SUPRATISHTHA VAJRAYE SVAHA

Cast the awareness flower with OM RATNA PUSHPE PRATICCHA HO

Give the secret name that accords with the family.

First is the Crown Empowerment fully adorned with the marks of the five families such as Vajrasattva and the others.

OM RATNA PUSHPE MALE ABHISHINCA HUM

Open the eye of ignorance with:

CAKSHU PRABESHAYA PHAT.

And explain the introduction to the mandala.

> Purifying all obscurations, liberation will be attained.

Samaya.

Second, the main part is conferring the empowerments.

Perform the meditation of the mandala deities and imagine that Vajrasattva confers the empowerments.

HUM

Within the space palace of the vase, awareness, the assemblies of peaceful and wrathful victorious ones melt into light. With this wisdom nectar, empowering the fortunate child, may all impure perceptions be purified and the nature of vessel and its contents be pure.

AKSHOBHYA KALASHA ABHISHINCA HUM.

The water fills your body and purifies stains. Imagine that the skandha of consciousness is transmuted, the mirror-like wisdom is realized, and the seed of accomplishing Vajra Akshobhya is planted in your being.

The residual of the water overflows, crowned with the victorious ones of the five families. Imagine that you thereby, obtain the wisdom crown.

SVA

From the nature of the five wisdoms, by adorning the noble child with the head ornament with the five families of jinas, may the wealth of wisdom be fully completed.

RATNASAMBHAVA MUKUTA ABHISHINCA TRAM.

Imagine that the skandha of sensation is transmuted, the wisdom of equality is realized, and the seed of accomplishing Ratnasambhava is planted in your being.

Give the empowerment symbols, the vajra and bell.

HUM

The unchanging vajra wisdom conquers all kleshas and thoughts. The very nature of discrimination, the vajra empowerment, I give to you. HUM

PADMA DHARA VAJRA ABHISHINCA HRIH

Imagine that the skandha of concept is transmuted, the discriminating wisdom (is realized) and the seed of accomplishing Amitabha is planted in your being.

HUM

Within the state of emptiness, the various sounds of the phenomenal realm accomplish the two meanings of dharma. This bell empowerment I give to you.

KARMA AMOGHASIDDHI ABHISHINCA AH

Imagine that the skandha of formation is transmuted, the all-accomplishing wisdom (is realized) and the seed of accomplishing Amoghasiddhi is planted in your being.

Empower with the vajra name:

HUM

By conferring this supreme vajra empowerment, this son of the victorious one is Vajrasattva. The vajra name is proclaimed as the body. May empowerment for buddhahood be obtained.

OM VAJRASATTVA ABHISHINCA OM

Imagine that the skandha of form is transmuted, the dharmadhatu wisdom (is realized) and the seed of accomplishing Vairochana is planted in your being.

In this way, bestowing the benefitting empowerments makes the disciples suitable vessels for secrets.

Then, for the Body empowerment: Imagine that the assembly of peaceful deities abides in your heart, the wrathful assembly in your bone mansion, the assembly of the vidyadharas in your throat, and that the assembly of dakinis abides in your navel.

HUM

By conferring the empowerment of the nondual
    lord and lady,
And the chief of the mandala, Samantabhadra,
May the transmuted mind and object, doer and
    deed,
Be realized as inseparable space and awareness.

A A ABHISHINCA HUM

HUM

By conferring the empowerment of the lords and
    ladies of the five families,
May the transmuted five poisons and five elements
Be spontaneously present as the five wisdoms
And realized as the nature of the five lights.

OM HUM SVA AM HA. HUM LAM MAM PAM TAM.
ABHISHINCA HUM

HUM

By conferring the empowerment of the eight
    bodhisattvas,
May the eight gatherings be transmuted.
By conferring the empowerment of the eight
    female bodhisattvas,
May the eight objects be transmuted.

BODHICITTA ABHISHINCA HUM༔

HUM༔
By conferring the empowerment of the six munis,༔
May the six kleshas be transmuted,༔
The six paramitas be perfected,༔
And the benefits to beings be unceasing.༔

MAHA MUNE ABHISHINCA HUM༔

HUM.
By conferring the empowerments of the four
    gatekeepers,༔
May the four extremes, permanence, and
    nothingness, be purified.༔
By conferring the empowerments of the four
    female gatekeepers,༔
May the four places of rebirth be purified.༔

KRODHA KRODHI ABHISHINCA HUM༔

HUM༔
By conferring the empowerment of Chemchok,
    lord and lady,༔
Supreme sovereign of all the wrathful ones,༔
May all thoughts of grasping and fixation be
    liberated༔
And nondual wisdom be realized.༔

HUM HUM ABHISHINCA HUM ༔

HUM ༔
By conferring the empowerment of the five
    herukas,༔
May the five klesha poisons be liberated.༔

By conferring the empowerment of the five lady
   herukas,

May the fixation on the five elements as concrete
   be liberated.

HUM HUM ABHISHINCA HUM

HUM

By conferring the empowerment of the eight
   ladies of the places,

May the thoughts of the eight gatherings be
   liberated.

By conferring the empowerment of the eight
   ladies of the valleys.

May the eight impure objects be liberated.

HA HE ABHISHINCA HUM

HUM

By conferring the empowerment of the four
   female gatekeepers,

May the four extremes, permanence, and
   nothingness, be liberated.

JAH HUM BAM HO. ABHISHINCA HUM

HUM

By conferring the empowerment of the twenty-
   eight shvaris,

May kleshas, grasping, and fixation be liberated.

BHYO ABHISHINCA HUM

HUM

May the vidyadhara gurus of the three lineages

Bless all the fortunate ones.
May all impure perception be purified
And pure perception dawn.

MAHA GURU ABHISHINCA HUM

HUM
By conferring the empowerment of the dakas and
dakinis,
May everything be purified as male and female
deities.
May all the stains of the kleshas be purified
And dawn as wisdom.

DHEVA DHEVI DHAKI ABHISHINCA HUM

Imagine that the obscurations of your body are
purified,
You are empowered to meditate on the deity,
And the seed of appearance dawning as deities
Is planted in your being.

From the throat centers of all the assemblies of deities, man-
tra garlands and seed syllables descend like rainfall. Imagine
that they dissolve into the nadis of the disciples, and the supreme
empowerment of speech is obtained. Perform the recitation
transmission, the mantra list, and give the blessed mala.

HUM
The supreme speech of all the victorious ones,
Is the continuity of resounding emptiness,
    beyond arising and ceasing.
By conferring the empowerment of all the dharani
    mantras,
May sounds heard be realized as mantra.

VAJRA VAKA ABHISHINCA AH༔

Imagine that all the obscurations of speech are
    purified,༔
And the seed of realizing sound as mantra is
    planted in your being.༔

From the hearts of the assembled deities of peaceful
    and wrathful victorious ones,༔
Countless attributes are emanated.༔
In the instant they dissolve into your heart center༔
Remain in the state of nonthought༔
And rest evenly in the continuity༔
Of the self-occurring self-liberation of thoughts.༔

HUM༔

The Vajra Mind of all the victorious ones༔
Is aware emptiness, beyond arising, dwelling, and
    ceasing.༔
By conferring the empowerment of the vajra of
    Mind,༔
May luminosity dawn as wisdom.༔

VAJRA CITTA ABHISHINCA HUM༔

Imagine that by these enabling empowerments that
    accomplish the benefit of oneself,༔
Such as meditating on the form of the deities,༔
Reciting mantra, and resting in evenness,༔
All the obscurations of mind are purified,༔
And the seed of realizing luminosity as wisdom
Is planted in your being.༔
These are conferred upon the diligent ones.༔

Third are the concluding actions.⸖

The guru should explain the samayas in detail.⸖ All together the disciples should promise [to keep them], give thanks, and offer themselves as servants.⸖ Perform the concluding ritual of the mandala, dedicate the virtue, and make aspirations.⸖ With all actions perfected, it will be meaningful.⸖

Samaya.⸖

This procedure of empowerments, if conferred on a person possessing devotion, will grant the attainment of liberation.⸖ Conferring empowerment of meditation and recitation will grant subsequent attainment of all the siddhis of Body, Speech, and Mind.⸖

Therefore, this text, meaningful to encounter, was taught by me, Padmakara.⸖

Tsogyal respectfully wrote it down and buried it as a treasure for the sake of the future. When it meets the destined son, may it cause the secret doctrine to flourish and benefit whoever encounters it.⸖

Samaya⸖. Seal.⸖

I, Chokgyur Dechen Lingpa took this out from the Cave of Glowing Turquoise on the southern slope of Yegyal Namkhadzö at Lawa Kangchik in Kham and translated it from the yellow parchment in Orgyen Samten Ling at Rudam Snow Range.

Notes on *The Destroyer of All Evil Deeds and Obscurations* Empowerment

Kyabje Tulku Urgyen Rinpoche

In most empowerments, you begin by tossing the awareness flower into the mandala. This symbolizes that ignorance is to be purified in its ground. Ignorance is temporary. We don't maintain unawareness when entering the mandala. That is the principle of taking the flower between the two fingers, holding it, and offering it by tossing it onto the mandala (board). At the same time, this is also a way of identifying the deity with whom you have a karmic destiny or a link from past lives. Wherever the flower lands is due to the co-incidence of your aspiration and the circumstance of the empowerment. It will land on one of the buddha families, either buddha, vajra, ratna, padma, or karma, with which you have a particular karmic connection. All the deities are aspects of rigpa, the five buddha families are five different aspects or types of deities. By tossing the flower, you thus recognize with which aspect of the mandala you have a particular link. That is one purpose.

When speaking of the outer and inner manifestations of inner space or outer and inner luminosity, outer refers to the manifest, meaning the form-body—the levels of nirmanakaya and sambhogakaya—whereas the inner space or inner luminosity refers to the dharmakaya itself.

The crown empowerment is the first of all the empowerments. First, you offer the flower of awareness and receive the flower back again after it has landed on the deity. You put the flower on the crown of your head and, at the same time, imagine that the deity upon which the flower landed is now the crown-buddha, or lord of the family, residing on the [seat] at the same time that you receive the crown. This is the first among all initiations.

This is a way to identify the particular aspect of the buddha-family with whom you are connected. Usually, the mandala is made up of the five buddha families: buddha in the center, surrounded by vajra, ratna, padma, and karma (in the four cardinal directions.) In the four intermediate directions are four petals that symbolize the four activities. Sometimes the Master will say: "Your flower landed on the padma family. Your main characteristic corresponds with the padma family practices."

In this empowerment of *Kunzang Tuktig,*[56] the Heart Essence of *Samantabhadra,* the above is not done because the text states that Samantabhadra is the essence of the entire mandala, and whichever place your flower falls is one of the manifestations of Samantabhadra. The lord who encompasses all the different buddha families is, in terms of dharmakaya, Samantabhadra. In terms of form, he is Vajrasattva or Vajradhara. In this case, it says, "Whichever deity your flower lands upon, he or she is all aspects of, or various expressions of, either Vajrasattva or Samantabhadra." It says afterwards you can take Vajrasattva, who embodies all the Buddha families, as the chief deity. In the Sarma School, one would go into more detail and receive a specific name that refers to a particular Buddha family, but not in this case. Whichever of the different aspects is indicated, they are none other than the various expressions or manifestations of either Samantabhadra or Vajrasattva.

The dharmakaya of dharmakaya is Samantabhadra, the sambhogakaya of dharmakaya is Vajradhara, and the nirmanakaya aspect of dharmakaya is Vajrasattva. Whichever of these three names you use, it is perfectly fine. It doesn't make that much difference.

The crown empowerment is given in order to identify the deity. Take off the blindfold that symbolizes ignorance and pick up the knowledge flower. Toss it into the mandala to identify the deity. As soon as it is clear who that is, the flower is placed back on the crown of your head. You are told, "Now, this is your nature." That's the idea. That is why it is the very first of the series of empowerments, since the deity is rigpa. All deities of Buddhism are rigpa itself—they are knowledge, not ignorance. That's why one tosses the 'flower of rigpa' into the mandala.

Before any empowerment, you remove the blindfold to remove your ignorance, offer the flower of awareness to the deity of awareness, and see who that is. All the different deities are like the different facial expressions of Samantabhadra or Vajrasattva. Just understand this. They all have the same nature. First identify which deity you should accomplish. Then you are ready to receive empowerment for that deity.

The first empowerments are called 'the five knowledge empowerments.' You receive the water empowerment of Akshobhya, the crown of Ratnasambhava, the vajra and bell of Amitabha, the bell of Amogasiddhi, [the ringing of] the name bell of Vairochana. After those five, there are the body empowerment of all buddhas, the speech empowerment of all buddhas, and the mind empowerment of all buddhas. These are the empowerments for the Mahayoga aspects of Ati. Therefore, they are called 'the general empowerments.'

'The extraordinary empowerments' are those for ground, path, and fruition. The ground is the ground of primordial purity. The path empowerment is the empowerment for

Trekchö: recognize your own nature, decide on one point, and gain confidence in liberation. The fruition empowerment is for Tögal and includes the empowerment for the expression of awareness. Each aspect has a vase empowerment, secret empowerment, wisdom-knowledge empowerment, and word empowerment. As I mentioned earlier, these are the elaborate, the unelaborate, the very unelaborate, and the extremely unelaborate, according to the Dzogchen system.

The elaborate is the vase empowerment, the unelaborate is the secret empowerment, the very unelaborate is the wisdom-knowledge empowerment, and the extremely unelaborate is the word empowerment in the general system. For each of the three of ground, path, and fruition, there are these four aspects. For the ground, the four empowerments are complete; for the path, the four empowerments are complete; and for the fruition, the four empowerments are complete as well. That's how it is taught. In this way, the development stage is Mahayoga, the completion stage is Anuyoga, and the utter Great Completion is Atiyoga. These are the empowerments we received in the *Kunzang Tuktig* empowerment. That's why there were so many different ones.

Having received the general empowerments for Mahayoga, one is authorized or permitted to practice the daily sadhana. When I gave the empowerments for ground, path, and fruition, I had to chant *The Ultimate Activity of Vajrasattva* (*Kunzang Don Treng*) prior to that. It contains a complete sadhana itself, including a feast-offering, and ends with lines of auspiciousness. That is what the master has to practice.

Within that short chant of *The Ultimate Activity of Vajrasattva* [while the disciples all chant the Vajrasattva mantra], all the topics equal to the immense scriptures of Dzogchen are included; everything is complete in just that.

Responsibilities for the Lama and Student *

Kyakhab Dorje, the Fifteenth Karmapa

After arranging all the necessary articles, the lama needs to do the practice for the empowerment he or she is giving.

Having completed the preparation, which includes preparation of the shrine, there is the actual part, which has four sections.

The accomplishment and offering [sections] of the mandala [and] the intent of empowerment, are preceded by the Seven Lines and the Lineage Supplication. The visualization of the support for the accumulations is as follows:

> Invoked by the light rays of my heart center, Guru Samantabhadra and the assembly of peaceful and wrathful deities, surrounded by a circle of the Three Jewels, Three Roots, and guardians, manifest filling the expanse of the sky.

Imagining this, recite three times the refuge and bodhicitta according to the *Practice Manual of the Peaceful and Wrathful Ones, The Manifest Essence*, beginning with: NAMO In the empty essence, and so forth. Gather the accumulations by means of, "Vajra master, glorious buddha," and so forth. Cultivate the four immeasurables through: "May all sentient beings have happiness and be free from suffering. May they

---

* Here is an abridged version of the empowerment manual for *The Destroyer of All Misdeeds and Obscurations*. Although it includes only the general empowerment, it nevertheless reveals the complexity of such an endeavor. MBS

not lose happiness and have impartiality." With "JAH HUNG BAM HOH" imagine that the field of accumulation dissolves into yourself.

At this point, consecrate the cleansing water. Uphold your pride with VAJRA MAHA SHRI HERUKA KON HAM. Purify the hindrance-torma with RAM YAM KHAM. Consecrate and multiply it with OM AH HUNG HA HOH HRIH. Summon with SARVA BIGHANAN AKARSHAYA JAH. Distribute it with SARVA BIGHANAN BALINGTA KHAHI.

With HUNG: *Duality demons of ignorant confusion*, and so forth, command and expel the obstructing forces, erect the protection circle, perform the offering consecration, and having unfolded the structure of the three samadhis, visualize yourself as indivisible from the deity with the samadhi of appearance and existence perfected in the ground. Perform the sealing, the empowerment conferral, the invitation of the wisdom beings, the dissolution and causing them to permanently remain, the paying of homage and making offering, and then the praise.

At the end of that, with HUNG: *All sights [are the body of the peaceful and wrathful ones],*" and so forth, purify the realm of the world and its inhabitants with the radiation and absorption. Without straying from the vital point of the meaning, but regarding it as perfected into the mandala of the three vajras, recite the combined mantra of the peaceful and wrathful ones not less than five-hundred times. Also, consecrate the vase by the samadhi of perfection within the space of a single concentration, just like the simultaneous perfection of multiple images in a single mirror. If you are unable to do that, take the *dharani* cord and say:

Within the self-existing palace of the vase,
I invoke the visualized assembly of deities with
    light.
The bodhicitta streams of the bliss of their union
Flows together as the wealth of liberation through
    seeing, feeling, and tasting.

Visualizing in this way, recite the combined mantra not less than three hundred times. At the end, offer them water with the 'conch water of the three syllables' and dissolve them into light.

For the action vase, visualizing Vajrasattva by saying, OM VA-JRASATTVA AH, gather and dissolve the blessings and, together with the downpour and purification of nectar, recite the hundred syllable mantra many times and the quintessence mantra one hundred times. Finally, perform the dissolution and shaping [of subsequent practices].

Perform the torma ritual for the Kama and Terma guardians. As for the cleansing, purification, and feast offering consecration, say:

RAM YAM KHAM
Vidyadhara gurus of the mind, sign, and hearing
    lineages,
And inseparable gatherings of yidams, dakinis,
    and dharma protectors,
Come, consider your great vajra samaya
Of the sense pleasures of united objects and sense
    organs.
OM AH HUNG VAJRA GURU VIDYADHARA SHANTA
KRODHA DAKINI DHARMAPALA

SAPARIVARA E A RALLI HRING HRING PHEM PHEM
JAH JAH.

Separating the first part of the feast articles into three aspects, first is presenting the outer, inner, and secret offering as the feast of sense pleasures:

OM AH HUNG
The samaya of the buddhas, the five meats and
    five nectars,
Is an ocean-like cloud of sense pleasures, the vajra
    enjoyments.
May this delightful feast offering of the union of
    bliss and emptiness
Be pleasing to the entire mandala of the three
    roots.
OM AH HUNG SARVA GANA CAKRA MAHA SUKHA
SAMAYA HOH.

Next is presenting the special unexcelled inner offering, and confessing violations and breaches:

HOH
All the faults and downfalls of our transgressing
    the vows and samayas
Due to ignorance, disturbing emotions,
    carelessness, and disrespect,
Since beginningless time until now,
We amend and confess with an ocean-like offering
    of sense pleasures.
OM VAJRA SAMAYA SHUDDHE A.

Last is the offering of freeing grasping and fixation, and of uniting wisdom and space:

Place the mental support substance before you [in] the triangle-shaped fire pit by saying E and visualize the aimed object with NRI TRI SARVA SHATRUM BIGHANAN. Summon with A KARSHAYA JAH. Call, bind, chain, and intoxicate with JAH HUNG BAM HOH. Conclude with PHAT. Complete all these actions and pierce with the action dagger:

> HUNG
> Amidst appearance and existence as the wrathful E
>   gathering,
> The servant of the Blazing One summons and
>   dissolves enemies and destructing forces.
> Sending their consciousnesses into the
>   dharmadhatu and reducing their physical body
>   to dust,
> They are arranged as the delightful substances for
>   eating flesh and drinking blood.
> SARVA SHATRUM BIGHANAN JAH HUNG BAM HOH.
> E YAM SPHARANA PHAT. MARAYARBAD.
> MAMSA RAKTA KIMNIRITI GANA CAKRA KHA KHA
>   KHAHI KHAHI.

Present the liberated flesh, blood, and bones. Elevate as nectar.

Then, the amendment of heart samaya:

> HUNG HRIH.
> I amend, proffer, and offer to you.
> May the heart samaya be amended ...
> The heart samayas being amended,
> I confess breaches, evil deeds, and failings.
> Please bestow the supreme and common siddhis.

First, for the entering:

Washing,
Boundary,
Mandala,
Applying the clothing,
Supplicating,
Purifying mind,
Taking the samaya pledge,
Giving water,
Taking oath,
Purifying the six realms,
Bringing down wisdom,
Stabilizing,
Tossing the flower,
Opening the eyes,
Disclosing the mandala.

Thus, there are fifteen steps.*

1. Let all the disciples be washed outside the gate by the action-vajra-master.
2. As above, offer the hindrance-torma and visualize the protection circle.
3. Having completed the distribution and collection of flowers, say:

> Listen, having strongly formed the precious bodhi-chitta attitude of thinking: "All sentient beings, filling space, have been our parents throughout our countless lifetimes. All these kind beings, tied by

---

* The fifteenth comes in a section not included here.

the shackle of confused thoughts, suffer terribly by undergoing the causation of total samsaric misery and have no opportunity for emancipation. I, alone, must quickly establish them in permanent happiness, the state of omniscience. In order to do that, I will enter the gate of the instructions of the Great Perfection and within this very life take hold of the permanent domain of Samantabhadra. I will, therefore, first request the profound empowerments that bring my being to maturation."

The ultimate entrance door to the entire ocean of teachings that illustrate the excellent path of complete liberation is the empowerment into the mandala of the Single Sphere of Ati, the secret cycle— or Instruction Section—among the three cycles or sections of the divisions of the Great Perfection that arose spontaneously through the compassionate power of Samantabhadra Vajradhara.

Among the numerous traditions of Kama, Terma, Pure Visions, and so forth, this is a cycle of the profound and extensive Earth Treasures. Moreover, among the different systems of all the accomplished masters that have appeared, this is the one belonging to the great master Padmakara of Uddiyana, the single embodiment of the wisdom of all buddhas ...

Thinking of the benefit for the future, he concealed the major part of his oral transmission as profound treasures. Thus, he unlocked the gate of his life example and buddha activity. In particular, concerning this teaching cycle manifesting the heart essence of Samantabhadra, the instruction like refined gold, which is the quintessence of all the teaching cycles of the Great Perfection, the *Döntri* says:

Here I will explain, in terms of ground, path, and
    fruition,⸪
The quintessential self-luminous wisdom-mind,⸪
Which is the Heart Essence of Samantabhadra,⸪
Belonging to the wish-fulfilling direct instruction⸪
Of the Instruction Section of the Great
    Perfection...⸪

As he so stated, it is an extremely special instruction,
complete and concise, that he bestowed upon the Chief of
Dakinis, Yeshe Tsogyal, and upon Prince Damdzin and his
consort as a personal sublime teaching. The root text says:

In this way, these ultimate instructions
Of extreme secrecy,⸪
Will, at the ultimate end of this age,⸪
Spread the heart teachings of Samantabhadra.⸪
The victorious ones have said that the Dzogchen
    instructions
Will liberate whomever encounters them.⸪
Therefore I, Padma, composed this
For the benefit of those many fortunate ones.⸪
Tsogyal wrote it down with devotion
And concealed it as a treasure for the sake of the
    destined one.⸪
May it cause the heart teachings of
    Samantabhadra
To be spread in all directions.⸪
Samaya, seal, seal, seal.⸪

Thus, he praised it and made aspirations. This teaching
was taken out by the Chakravartin of the ocean of treasure
revealers, Orgyen Chokgyur Dechen Lingpa, at Lawa Kang-

chik in Kham, from the Cave of the Turquoise Turtle on the southern slope of Yegyal Namkhadzo.

This teaching cycle of *The Pure Gold Great Perfection, the Sacred Teaching Heart Essence of Samantabhadra* has two sections: the ripening empowerments and liberating instructions. Within these are the general Ati mandala of the peaceful and wrathful ones, the benefiting empowerments of accepting the devoted ones, and the enabling empowerments for the industrious ones. By means of the special *Ultimate Empowerment Wish-fulfilling Jewel* there are the ground empowerments of primordial purity and spontaneous presence, the path empowerments for those of sharp faculties to enter Trekchö, and the fruition (empowerments) of entering the Tögal essence for those with the most excellent faculties.

Among these different ripening and freeing transmissions, the first is to accept the devoted and industrious ones, conferring the empowerment of *The Destroyer of All Misdeeds and Obscurations,* ripening [those accepted] into the Ati-Maha mandala of the peaceful and wrathful victorious ones. For this, the master has completed the actions to be done beforehand, such as perfecting the mandala, making offerings, and so forth. Now it will be transmitted to all of you as your good fortune.

Additionally, there are acts for the disciples to perform.

4. Since, until now, you have been blinded by the obscuring veil of not seeing your natural face, as a symbol of not seeing the primordially existing real mandala, bind your face and cover your eyes with the red gauze band. A KHAM VIRA HUNG.

Now, as the symbolic gift of meeting the primordially existing mandala of self-display, imagine that you are holding up, in your hands, a garland of supreme udumvara flowers of five colors. A KHAM VIRA HUNG.

5. With the respectful frame of mind of being in the presence of the vajra master seated [before you], in the form of Samantabhadra Vajradhara, the embodiment of all the victorious ones, repeat this supplication:

> HO.
> Guru, glorious Vajrasattva,
> Please regard us with loving kindness.
> Lead us out samsara
> And let us enter the citadel of liberation.

Repeat this three times, as in *The General Procedure of Empowerments, the Destroyer of All Evil Deeds and Obscurations.*

6. In order to take refuge, which is the basis for all vows, it is first necessary to become a suitable vessel for the empowerments. In the presence of the guru, the assembly of mandala deities, and the circle of the three roots and victorious ones—who are seated in the manner of being self-manifested from the expression of essence, nature, and capacity—with the one-pointed aspiration of taking the true refuge beyond the views and meditations of the vehicles of mental fabrication, repeat this:

> NAMO.$_o^o$
> In the empty essence, dharmakaya...$_o^o$
> I take refuge until enlightenment.$_o^o$

Repeat this three times, as in The Manifest Essence Practice Manual.

In order to arouse the intent on supreme enlightenment, the highway of all vows, think: "Taking all my mother sentient beings equal to the sky out of samsara's ignorance and confused thinking, I will establish them in the state of the perfectly enlightened Samantabhadra. To do that, I will receive the ripening and freeing transmission that authorizes me to practice the instructions of the Great Perfection! With this thought, arouse bodhicitta and repeat this:

> HO
> In order to establish all beings equal to the sky
> In the state of buddhahood,
> I will realize the dharmakaya of self-existing
>   awareness
> Through the teachings of the Great Perfection.

Repeat this three times.

In order to gather the accumulations, which are the conducive conditions for swiftly gaining the realization of the profound path, in the presence of these supreme fields, while vividly recalling the meaning of each of the eight branches— that is, the condensed essence of accumulation and purification—repeat this:

Vajra master, glorious buddha and so forth.

Repeat three times.

As the foundation of the path—the tantric vows of the vidyadharas—today take the general trainings of Vinaya,

Abhidharma, and in particular, the samayas of the guru's Body, Speech, and Mind, in the presence of the guru and the entire assembly of mandala deities. With the firm resolve to never give them up even at the cost of your life, repeat this:

> HO.
> Sugatas, peaceful and wrathful victorious ones,
>   please consider me.
> From now until supreme enlightenment,
> I will not abandon the samayas of Body, Speech
>   and Mind,
> Even at the cost of my life.

Repeat this three times, as in the empowerment text *The Destroyer of All Evil Deeds and Obscurations.*

7. As it is necessary to keep the series of samayas—the life-force of empowerment—which you have here promised to hold, without violations, imagine that the vajra water that discriminates between keeping and transgressing dissolves into the center of your heart. Take the oath water by uttering the three syllables and saying:

> HO.
> By remaining in the continuity of Body, Speech,
>   and Mind,
> I will accomplish all the siddhis.
> If I do not keep it, I will be reborn in the hells.
> Therefore, I shall keep the samayas.
> OM AH HUNG VAJRA KA VA CI SAMAYA RAKSHA
>   TISHTHA

Then place the vajra at the three places

8. Arouse the firm intelligence of never transgressing the series (of samayas) that were proclaimed here and which you have promised to keep by taking the oath of the vajra pledge. Say,

SAMAYA IDAN NARAKAN

9. For the purpose of purifying your evil deeds and obscurations along with your mass of defilements, the seeds which throw you into the wheel of the six realms of samsara, visualize in the center of each of the chakras of nadi-knots within your body, the objects of purification which are the seed syllables of the six realms. Visualize, upon each of them a set of the three purifying seed syllables, as follows:

> Above the head, in the throat, in the heart center,
> In the navel, in the secret place, and in the soles of the feet,
> Are A, SU, NRI, TRI, PRE, and DU, upon which
> The actual form of the Body, Speech and Mind of the victorious ones...
> Is drawn down by the syllables RAM, YAM and KHAM...

Visualized in this way, from the purifying syllable RAM appears wisdom fire which, starting from the soles of your feet, step by step burns away the seeds along with your evil deeds, obscurations, and habitual patterns. The wind of dharmata from YAM scatters away all the ashes. Then visualize that the water of compassion from KHAM washes away all the defilements of your habitual patterns so that they are permanently gone.

RAM SAPHARANA PHAT
YAM SAPHARANA PHAT
KHAM SAPHARANA PHAT

Recite this triple-element mantra at the beginning of each of the six sets of mantras beginning with OM DAHA DAHA:

OM DAHA DAHA SARVA NARAKA GATE HETUM HUNG PHAT

OM PACA PACA SARVA PRETAKA GATE HETUM HUNG PHAT

OM MATHA MATHA SARVA TIRYAKA GATE HETUM HUNG PHAT

OM CACHINDHA CACHINDHA SARVA NRI GATE HETUM HUNG PHAT

OM TRATA TRATA SARVA ASURA GATE HETUM HUNG PHAT

OM BHRITA BHRITA SARVA SURA GATE HETUM HUNG PHAT

By having purified your defilements, along with your habitual patterns in this way, imagine that your body has the nature of a pure and brilliant mass of light.

10. In order to bring down the resplendence, vividly visualize the form of Shri Vajrasattva, Lord of the Mandala, in this way:

From the state of emptiness, upon a lotus and
    moon,
Is the white bhagavan Vajrasattva,
Holding vajra and bell, seated in half-vajra
    posture, and visualized as ornamented with silks
    and jewels.

His three places are marked with OM AH HUNG.
The inconceivable wisdom gatherings of Body,
   Speech, and Mind
Of all the assemblies of mandala deities
Are emanated and absorbed.
OM AH HUNG JNANA KAYA VAKA CHITTA ABESHAYA
A AH

Bring down the resplendence by means of mantra, incense, music, and samadhi.

11. Invoked in this way, the stream of blessing of the
   wisdom aspect remains firm in constant changelessness.
   While uttering OM SUPRATISHTHA VAJRAYE SVAHA, seal
   with the vajra in the manner of making the gesture of a
   cross.
12. In order to discover the predestined deities of your
   family, as you offer the previously given flower to this
   mudra-mandala—which is the mandala where the
   groups of the peaceful and wrathful sugatas of the
   five families abide as vivid perfection—think, "May
   whichever deity that I have been linked to for lifetimes
   accept this!" Swear to this, commit yourself, and offer
   the flower while repeating the following:

   OM RATNA PUSHPE PRATICCHA HO.

Make certain as to which of the different families [it falls]
and don the flower as the sign of empowerment.

Or, in the general manner: With the flower landing on
the main figure of the mandala—since the guru is not different from Samantabhadra Vajrasattva—you are given Va-

jrasattva Dechen Dupa Tsal as your secret name. The flower itself, blessed with the nature of the chief of the family, is the first of the empowerments, the conferring of the flower-crown empowerment.

Additional prayers inserted.

13. Imagine that from the heart center of the vajra master a ray of light like a golden spoon appears directly and removes the obscuration of co-emergent ignorance, symbolized by the eye-band. Say:

CHAKSHU PRABESHAYA PHAT

14. By obtaining the eye of wisdom in this way, (you perceive) all the deities of the self-existing ultimate mandala, demonstrated by the symbolic examples, the material mandala of concrete signs. That is to say, upon the elements and Mount Sumeru, which are the mandalas of the dhatus of the five consorts who are the pure aspects of the elements that create the world of existence, and within the dome of fire, weapons, and vajras, which burn away fixation on concreteness and protect against conceptual thoughts; there are the lotus of non-attachment, the charnel grounds of the eight purified gatherings, and the immeasurable palace of the purified skandhas. It is the immeasurable palace of the great liberation with the unfabricated and spontaneously perfected decoration of the qualities of ground, path, and fruition, such as the thirty-seven factors of enlightenment and the four wisdoms of the purified four notions, and other objects of purification.

Within its upper story are the peaceful sambhogakaya deities. In its lower story is the mandala of the wrathful manifestations, with assemblies of vidyadharas, gurus, dakas, dakinis, and dharma protectors. Like the sun and its rays, the single wisdom unobstructedly manifests as the realm of the three kayas. By the power of witnessing the actual presence of this vivid and perfect mandala with palace and deities, imagine that within the celestial palace of your body you are meeting the deities of the mandala of the three vajras, which fundamentally exists within yourself since the beginning.

And so, the topics for entering the mandala are completed. Concerning the actual empowerment, there are the benefiting [empowerments] and the enabling [empowerments]:

First is the sequential conferral of the five benefiting empowerments to the devoted ones by means of the outer empowerment articles: water, crown, vajra, bell, and name …

While ringing the name-bell above their heads, say:

SHINCA OM SHRI HERUKA VAJRASATTVA MAHASUKHA
PRAJNA NAMA BHAVATI HO.

In this way, these empowerments have completely purified the mass of disturbing emotions and the mind streams of the disciples which they realize to be wisdom. They are made suitable vessels for the secret mandala and so are benefited. Therefore, the renowned five benefiting empowerments are completed.

Second comes the sequential conferral of the 'enabling empowerment of action' to the industrious ones by means of the symbols of body, speech, and mind: bodily forms, mantra inscription, and attributes. Of these three, the first is the body empowerment …

Since you are enabled to engage in the practice steps of purifying body, speech, and mind into the three vajras, that which is renowned as the three inner enabling empowerments is completed.

The conclusion of the empowerments

Although, in this way, you have obtained the blessing through the empowerments, whether or not it is retained in your being depends on the samayas. Therefore, it is necessary to correctly keep the different disciplines of the Vajrayana tripitaka and especially the condensed samayas. So, take to heart the pledge of acting accordingly and repeat:

As the master has proclaimed and so forth …

Thus, the devoted ones have been accepted and have completely received The Destroyer of All Misdeeds and Obscurations, the general empowerments that authorize you to visualize and recite the mantra. Now offer a mandala as a gift of thanks for this kindness.

… With the body-offering and so forth, conclude in the general way.

[The Colophon]*

---

*Included here is the colophon for the entire manual, which is three times as long as this excerpt.

Offered as fulfillment of the request from the nirman-akaya Samten Gyatso, the sacred holder of the dharma and the family lineage of the incarnated great treasure revealer and lord of the dharma; and as a necessity for and in service to this supreme and precious teaching, it was completed on the thirteenth day of the waxing part of the ninth month of the Raudra year [October 25, 1920] by the venerable vidyadhara Kunsang Khakyab Dorje who is included at the end of the line of incarnations of Buddha Karmapa, at the spontaneously accomplished palace of the practice center Samten Yi-ong Ling situated at the hermitage of Tsur Dowo Lung, near the great Garuda Fortress Splendorous Cave. The second copy was written out by the learned monk Lama Jampal Tsultrim. May virtuous goodness increase.

Empowerment and Samaya *

Orgyen Tobgyal Rinpoche

Whether you enter the path of Vajrayana depends on whether you have received empowerment or not. When you receive an empowerment, it is necessary to do the practice for that empowerment. The lineage empowerment is first, followed by the path empowerments, which all together authorize disciples to do the practices. The path vase empowerment is for the practice of the development stage. The path secret empowerment is for the practices of nadis, prana, and bindus, as well as mantra recitation. The path wisdom-knowledge empowerment utilizes the emptiness of the example wisdom to encourage the ultimate wisdom being to arise in your experience. The secret and the wisdom-knowledge empowerments correspond to the completion stage with and without characteristics respectively. The precious word empowerment authorizes you to practice Dzogchen, primordially pure Trekchö and spontaneously present Tögal.

The best disciples will maintain an unbroken flow. Immediately upon receiving this empowerment, they will instantly be undeluded, undistracted, and practice the path. The middling ones can maintain awareness six times in a day. Those with lesser capacity will hold this awareness at least one time each day. This is the process of receiving the four empowerments for yidam practice. You must practice until you truly actualize the result of the path, without breaking the continuity of the deity.

---

*Translated by Gyurme Avertin and Marcia B. Schmidt

After you receive the lineage empowerment, utilize the deity empowerment and do not abandon sadhana practice. If you practice the deity after receiving the lineage empowerment, ultimately you will become enlightened while temporarily you will receive the fruition empowerment. The fruition empowerment bestows all the qualities of the three kayas of buddhahood. At that point, you will effortlessly benefit innumerable sentient beings as vast as the sky. I have given this condensed explanation of empowerment so you can understand. Merely receiving empowerment from a lama has a bit of benefit, but without practicing, you will not become enlightened...

Just receiving empowerments and listening to teachings are not the most important things. Most vital is to practice and accomplish what you receive. Once you follow the Vajrayana path—where you receive empowerments and teachings and practice development and completion—it will not be long before you attain the state of buddhahood. Practice is essential.

SAMAYA

The life-force of the empowerment is the samaya. There are samayas of body, speech, and mind; the twenty-five samayas; and the one hundred thousand samayas. Having gotten an empowerment, people sometimes say, "Oh, don't talk about the samayas, because people will be freaked out." That is the worst thing I've ever heard, because that's a one-way ticket to hell, for sure.

As for the samayas, we don't keep most of them actually. In general, that's the situation: we actually break more samayas than we keep. That is why Vajrasattva gave the hundred syllable mantra, which is the most powerful way of restoring samayas. Vajrasattva himself said that if you recite the hundred syllable mantra one hundred and eight times without distraction, then all the negativity, all the samaya breakages you may have done, will all be cleansed and purified. Vajrasattva is not a liar. That means that reciting this mantra has enormous benefit. However, first you need to be able to do it well, correctly. What is difficult is to be undistracted—which basically means you recite the mantra, visualize the deity, think of the meaning, and leave the mind undistracted. If, on the other hand, you recite the mantra and you're just thinking of all sorts of things, that's when the mind is distracted.

The root of empowerment is samaya, as I have said, and there are two categories, the root and subsidiary—or branch—samayas. There are fourteen root samayas. The first is to not go against the vajra master,[57] upset or disobey him or her. The lama is the vajra master. The vajra master can be endowed with one, two, or three kindnesses. The first kindness pertains to the master who bestows empowerment. Having given empowerment, the master with the second kindness also explains the tantras. A master who points out the nature of mind is endowed with the third kindness. We need to cherish the master endowed with the three kindnesses more than our own hearts. It is your choice whether you cherish the lama It is necessary to check the master before you receive teachings from him or her, and that is about merely receiving any teachings. Regarding empowerments, it is more critical to check the teacher; you need to make sure that he or she has the proper lineage. To be introduced to mind's nature in Dzogchen, then you really need to investigate the master giving these teachings.

When receiving the vows of the lower vehicle, you are like a child, and the abbot who imparts them is like your father. Buddha Shakyamuni said this in the Vinaya. When you receive the trainings of Mahayana, the lama is like a doctor and the student is like a sick person. If you do not take the medicine and the doctor's advice, you die. For an empowerment, you need to see the master as indivisible from [the main deity of] the mandala, which is the way to receive the empowerment. If not, you will not really get the empowerment. To truly receive the pointing out instruction, you need to see the master as the Buddha. If you see the teacher as the Buddha, you can be introduced to the mind as the Buddha. This teacher is the most precious and important.

Then there are the samayas of the three kayas, and if you go against them, you break them. So, the second root samaya is to abide by whatever instruction the teacher gives you.

The third root samaya concerns dharma friends[58] and there is a lot to say about this. In fact, buddha nature permeates all beings; we all have the same basis. Merely harming even one sentient being is a negative action. That is the larger dharma community. A smaller group would be the students of the same teacher. Even closer are those with whom you receive empowerment in one mandala. It becomes increasingly tighter as you receive not only an empowerment but teachings together as well. Then there are those with whom you receive Dzogchen teachings and they are truly your vajra siblings. They are very important and to be treated with respect. There are many texts that explain this. It says that you need to consider each one of them as the lama, and it explains why you should avoid fighting with them in any manner, not even holding negative thoughts about them in your mind. There are many details and if you do not keep them, you will go to hell. Actually, you will go to the worst hell. In Sutra it is called Avichi Hell; in Vajrayana, it is called Vajra Hell. And you will stay there a very long time, an immeasurable length of time.

These days, people do not respect these [samayas] at all. They do try somewhat to keep the samayas with the lama, as long as there are no difficulties. Mentally, you probably do think negative things about the lama. But there is no consideration whatsoever for vajra siblings. That is only the third [root samaya], so you can imagine the rest!

What do you do when samayas are broken? There are several levels [of breakage], according to time: damaged, transgressed, and broken. The quicker you can purify it through confession, the better. Time matters; it matters how long it has been damaged, whether it is a month, days, or weeks. We have the way to confess as illustrated in different practices.

I mentioned reciting the Vajrasattva mantra as one way. Feast offering is a supreme way to purify breakages and remain clean. We need to accumulate both merit and wisdom, and feast offering increases these. Therefore, we make offerings to the dharma.

Explaining the Life-force, the Samayas

The *Lamrim Yeshe Nyingpo* root text says:

> The samaya vows are the life-force of
>   empowerment.⸖
> With the pledge to not transgress the discipline of
>   Mantra,⸖
> Keep purely, in the outer, inner, and secret ways,⸖
> The samayas comprised of the general, special, and
>   supreme types.⸖

Though your stream-of-being has been ripened by empowerment, the samaya is the life-force that preserves the nature of that empowerment within your being.

That is to say, you obtain the samayas and precepts simply by having had empowerment conferred and therefore must carefully maintain them.[59] The Assemblage says:

> By fully completing the empowerments
> One should observe without any violation
> All the root and branch samayas.
> Through that, the supreme accomplishment will
>   be attained.

THE IDENTITY OF SAMAYA

Samaya is the attitude that does not transgress the particular points to be observed, together with the source of that attitude. *The Subsequent Essence Tantra* describes this:

The one who persistently keeps the samayas
Will observe them even in dreams.
Taking a pledge is regarded as the [binding] vow.

Hence it is samaya in terms of adhering to, and keeping without violation, the three vajra-secrets of all the buddhas, while it is precept in terms of controlling one's stream-of-being.[60] It is therefore a single identity which is distinguished in terms of its particular or general aspects.

THE DEFINITION OF SAMAYA

It is called the Vinaya of Mantra, because, having entered through the door of Mantra, it tames the disturbing emotions of one's stream-of-being through observing its discipline and through practicing.

The word *samaya* means 'pledged commitment,' 'oath,' 'precept,' etc. Hence it is a vajra promise or samaya[61] because one is not to transgress what one has pledged. Samaya involves both benefit and risk because if kept, the samaya becomes the foundation for all the trainings of Mantra; if not kept, all the trainings become futile. *The Heruka Assemblage Tantra* states:

The supreme bind is to never transgress.
If transgressed, it is taught that one will be
        burned.[62]

THE DIVISIONS OF SAMAYAS

The Tantra of the Assemblage of Peaceful Sugatas says:

> They should be observed after classifying them
> Into general, special, and supreme [samayas].

Hence, they are comprised of three types: the general samayas, the special samayas, and the supreme samayas. These should be observed and kept pure in the manner of regarding them outwardly as your heart, inwardly as the blood in your heart, and innermostly as your life-force.[63]

When describing the meaning of samaya in more detail, the general samayas are renowned as the observances of the pratimoksha, the bodhisattva [trainings], and the three outer tantras. The first of these is what should be adopted or avoided regarding the eight sets of Individual Liberation. The second consists of the trainings within the traditions of the two chariots. The third includes all the general and particular samayas found in the Kriya, Charya, and Yoga tantras.[64]

The special samayas are the common samayas of the five families taught in Anuttara Mantra as well as all the special samayas comprised of the root and branches.[65]

THE SAMAYAS OF THE FIVE FAMILIES

1) The samaya of the Tathagata family is, externally, the bodhichitta of aspiration and application, and the three disciplines of constraining [oneself from misdeeds], practicing [virtue], and benefiting [others];[66] as well as adherence to the Three Jewels; and, as the hidden meaning, to adhere to

the bodhichitta of indivisible bliss and emptiness and to the mind-essence having the nature of the Three Jewels.

2) The samaya of the Vajra family is, externally, to keep the material vajra and bell, and to adhere to the mahamudra of the form of the deity; internally, to adhere to union by sealing the secret spheres of the lord and lady; secretly, to adhere to union by sealing the two white and red elements with blazing and dripping; and, as thatness, to bind bliss and emptiness with the seal of unity. Thus, it requires adherence to the outer, inner, secret vajra and bell, and the three mudra-seals, as well as adhering respectfully to the master who teaches these points.

3) The samaya of the Ratna family is, externally, the four types of giving: the generosity of dharma, protection, and material things[67] as well as their root, loving kindness; and, as the hidden meaning, the giving of the wisdoms of the four joys of descending and ascending bodhichitta by means of the fire of passion.

4) The samaya of the Padma family is adherence to the three vehicles: externally shravaka, and pratyekabuddha; internally bodhisattva; secretly Kriya, Charya, and the outer and inner Yoga; and, as the hidden meaning, the practice of the indestructible speech by binding the pranas within the central channel.[68]

5) The samaya of the Karma family is to practice, as much as one is able, all of the former precepts as well as the actions of offering.[69] Concerning the sentient beings who need to be guided further [on the path], the samaya is to deliver all those who have not been delivered, to free all those who have not been freed, to confirm all those who have not been confirmed, and to establish in transcendence all those who have fully transcended misery.[70] The hidden meaning is to

seal everything with the binding of E and VAM union, as well as making satisfying offerings to the divinities of the aggregates, elements, sense faculties and sense objects with the melting bliss. It also is to deliver, free, confirm, and transcend the gross and subtle three doors into the nature of the extremely subtle three vajras, the great primordially liberated basic perfection.[71]

THE ROOT SAMAYAS

In general, the samayas of body, speech, and mind are to turn away from nonvirtue in thought, word, and deed, and not to deviate from deity, mantra, and samadhi.

In particular, the samaya of the Vajra-Body consists of two actions. First, to serve your master with whatever is pleasing, without any deceit in your thoughts, words, and deeds. Second, not to sever yourself from your dharma friends, but to act kindly with unceasing affection and an attitude of benefiting them.

The samaya of the Vajra-Speech is, corresponding to whether your diligence is of a higher or medium level, not to neglect the mantra and mudra during the six periods of day and night[72] or on the special days, months, and years.

The samaya of the Vajra-Mind is to refrain from divulging the secret meaning to others and not to deviate from the mudra of union, the unexcelled bodhichitta.

Specifically, the samaya of great equality is to evenly unite with the Body, Speech and Mind of all buddhas because all beings are natural purity since the beginning. Endeavor in that since all siddhis result from realizing and growing familiar with it through discriminating knowledge and samadhi.

The five sets of five branch samayas:

1) The 'five to recognize' are to realize that all the fivefold conceptions, such as the aggregates and elements, are primordially a mandala of kayas and wisdoms, such as the five male and female buddhas, and so forth. This is the samaya of the view.[73]

2) The 'five not to be rejected' are not to abandon the five poisons because they become helpers to the path when embraced by skillful means. According to the hidden meaning, delusion is the view free from partiality and the action free from differentiating through acceptance and rejection; desire is the great nonconceptual compassion; anger is self-knowing wakefulness which conquers conceptual thinking; pride is the king of the view of unity which does not 'cave in;' and envy is to not allow thoughts that cling to dualistic fixation any room within the expanse of equality. By means of the practice of realizing and growing familiar with them, they should not be rejected.

3) The 'five to be undertaken' are to take life, to take what is not given, to engage in sexual misconduct, to lie, and to utter harsh words, when they are for the benefit of others, such as delivering the ten objects.[74] According to the hidden meaning [these five are] to interrupt the pranas, the life-force, by such means as the vase-shaped [breathing], or to cut the life-force of dualistic thinking by means of self-knowing wakefulness; to take the shukra of the queen or the wisdom of great bliss that is not given by anyone; to practice the unchanging melting bliss by means of uniting self-knowing with the object of Mahamudra, which is sexual misconduct; to deliver sentient beings from a samsara that is

a nonexistent presence, which is lying; and to talk without concealment or secrecy through realizing all sounds to be inexpressible, which is harsh words.

4) The 'five to accept' are to partake of the essences of red and white bodhichitta, excrement, urine, and human flesh for the purpose of purifying concepts of clean and unclean. According to the hidden meaning, this means enjoying the essences of the five aggregates by binding them to be undefiling.[75]

5) The 'five to be cultivated' are to correctly cultivate in one's stream-of-being the five samayas to recognize by means of the application of realizing and growing familiar with them. Hence, they are the samayas of meditation.

The middle three sets are chiefly the outer samayas of conduct. These three root samayas and twenty-five branch samayas are renowned in the general terminology of Mahayoga as the twenty-eight samayas.

THE SUPREME SAMAYAS

For the person who abides by these general and special samayas there are twenty extra samayas that are to be adhered to and observed at the time of sadhana, etc., such as not destroying the lion throne, and so forth. When making this indicated meaning more comprehensible, they are as follows:

1) To not harm the body of the vajra master and to not break his command.
2) To not enjoy the master's consort.
3) To not refuse [the dharma to] a gathering of devoted people.

4) To not partake of the funds of the Three Jewels or of a pandita and to not drink liquor to [the point of] intoxication.
5) To not enjoy the consort of a vajra friend.
6) To not use an unqualified consort.
7) To not use unqualified samaya substances.
8) To *not belittle the qualities of a pandita.*
9) To not expound the secret teachings to an unworthy recipient.
10) To not reject a qualified consort.
11) To not reject a worthy disciple.
12) To not part from the meaning of bliss and emptiness or from the symbolism of lord and lady.
13) To not fight with a dharma friend, even in jest.
14) To not use the residual [feast articles] offered by another.
15) To not crave for the throne of a master.
16) To not break the retreat of self and others.
17) To not let samadhi be overtaken by dullness and agitation and to not interrupt recitation and ritual with ordinary talk.
18) To not transgress the seal or the sign of empowerment and to not forget the symbolism.
19) To not disturb the mandala of a yogi and to not retaliate against spells cast by ordinary people.
20) To not give up respecting the master at the crown of one's head.

THE METHOD OF OBSERVING THE SAMAYAS

The samayas should be observed assiduously by the following means: the perfect mindfulness of the points of permission and prohibition; the conscientiousness of examining whether or not the samayas have been transgressed; the carefulness of being attentively on guard; the conscience of shunning violations if they do occur, by reproaching oneself; the embarrassment of shunning violations, by [being reproached by] other people; the fearfulness due to perceiving the defects of violations; and the respect due to delighting in the benefits. This is described in the *Samvarodaya:*

> For the one who desires the supreme siddhi,
> It is easy to sacrifice even his life.
> It is also comfortable to arrive at the point of
>   death.
> So always observe the samayas.

RESTORING THE SAMAYAS WHEN VIOLATED

The samayas that have been violated in regard to a person should be apologized for to that person. All other violations should be apologized for in any suitable way by means of remorse and resolution. A major violation can even occur based on a 'light' object and should first of all be apologized for according to your respective tradition. Then, you should again receive empowerment and samaya.

If a follower of Mantra breaks ('gal) the root samayas, he will go directly to Vajra Hell. Indicated by this, there are such negative consequences from violations. On the other hand, if the samayas are observed correctly, it is taught that the temporary and ultimate benefits are immeasurable. The most eminent result will be accomplished at best within one lifetime, or, next best, within seven to sixteen lives.

Keeping Samayas

Kyabje Tulku Urgyen Rinpoche

As you know, there are different vehicles for shravakas, bodhisattvas, and followers of Secret Mantra. Each has their respective precepts, trainings, and samayas. When condensed into the essence, the very heart of all these samayas is contained in the four samayas of the Dzogchen view —nonexistence, all-pervasiveness, oneness, and spontaneous perfection—and the three root samayas of Body, Speech, and Mind. As Vajrayana practitioners, we abide by all these three sets of principles. For instance, we take refuge at the very beginning of any empowerment, and have therefore received the refuge precepts of the shravakas. After that, we form the bodhichitta resolve and so also receive the bodhisattva precepts. As for Secret Mantra, the moment we drink the 'samaya water,' the drops of water from the conch given out before the actual empowerment, the water is transformed into Vajrasattva, who rests in the center of our hearts. When we keep the samayas we are never separate from Vajrasattva.

A good way to describe Vajrayana samayas is to use the example of a snake in the hollow of a bamboo shaft. The snake can neither go right nor left; it must either go up or down. Going up describes what is called the 'upward directness' which indicates we are ready to enter a buddha-field. On the other hand, there is the 'downward directness' which applies to those who break the samaya vows. I hate to mention this, but such a person can only go downward into the three lower realms. This is precisely what is meant by the tremendous benefit or the correspondingly huge risks involved in the Vajrayana samayas. To be Vajrayana practitioners we must have received the four empowerments, which in themselves are the very heart of the path of Secret Mantra. We have entered the Vajrayana path simply by receiving these four empowerments. In other words, the snake has already crept into the bamboo shaft. If you keep the samayas, you gain supreme accomplishment. If not, then that which remained as Buddha Vajrasattva in the center of your heart as long as you observed the purity of samaya transforms itself into a 'fierce yaksha,' a [self-destructive] force that shortens your life-span and 'consumes the vital essences of your heart-blood.' This is the way to inescapably propel yourself into the downward directness at the end of your life.

The practice of Secret Mantra is the short-cut, the swiftest path to reaching the inconceivable common and supreme accomplishments. As you move up through the different vehicles, the 'narrow defile' of this path of samaya grows increasingly confined; there is less and less room to move, so be on guard. In the case of a shravaka or bodhisattva, it is simpler to progress: remain virtuous and disciplined in thought, word, and deed. [In other words,] stay on guard against unwholesome behavior and adopt what is good. The samayas of Vajrayana, on the other hand, are to never let your body depart from being the deity, your voice from being mantra, and your mind from the state of samadhi. If you are able to do so, that is keeping the ultimate samayas with the Body, Speech, and Mind of the victorious ones. You can then truly be said to possess the sacred precepts of Vajrayana. Without doing so, understand that the samayas of Secret Mantra hold extreme risk.

There are as well the samayas with the vajra master: to

not disparage his bodily presence, break his command, or upset his feelings.

Let me again summarize about the different samayas. Concerning your vajra master, do not disrespect his bodily presence, his word, or his feelings. Moreover, do not separate your body from being the deity, your voice from mantra, and your mind from samadhi.

As for 'vajra siblings,' there are three kinds: distant, close, and very close. The very close brothers and sisters are the ones together with whom you received instructions on mind essence at the feet of the same master. Close vajra siblings are the people with whom you have taken the same empowerments and oral instructions. The distant siblings are for instance, the people who were present in a huge dharma gathering or empowerment assembly, sometimes numbering into the thousands. We must keep our samaya with all these brothers and sisters, staying clear of perceiving them as imperfect, harboring resentment, ridiculing or belittling one another, criticizing behind each other's back, and the like. If you can remain completely unpolluted, without any of those defects, you can be said to have pure samaya.

Ultimately, to be totally free from any defects in your vows and samayas, you need to remain in the continuity of the four samayas of the Dzogchen view: nonexistence, all-pervasiveness, oneness, and spontaneous perfection. If you are able to fulfill these, you totally transcend any possible violation or breach of samaya. Nonexistence and all-pervasiveness are the two samayas of Trekchö, while oneness and spontaneous perfection are the samayas of Tögal. To accomplish these, you need to be able to dissolve dualistic mind into nondual awareness, rigpa.

This nondual awareness is the very identity of the three

kayas of the awakened state of buddhahood. Within it all three—dharmakaya, sambhogakaya and nirmanakaya—are complete. The three vajras of all buddhas—the unchanging Vajra Body, the unceasing Vajra Speech and the unmistaken Vajra Mind—are complete within it as well. When you remain in the fourfold samaya of nonexistence, all-pervasiveness, oneness, and spontaneous perfection, not a single infraction or transgression of samaya is possible, not even as much as a hair-tip. Until this point however, there is no avoiding incurring breaches of samaya, be they subtle or coarse.

In the general classifications of samaya, you find the four stages called infraction, transgression, violation, and breach [literally: contradicting, damaging, breaking, and passing]. These categories depend in part on the length of time which has passed since the samaya was damaged. After three years of still not having apologized, there is no longer any chance to mend the samaya. At this point it is overstepped and becomes irreparable.

The precepts and trainings of the Sutra system, including both Hinayana and Mahayana, are difficult to repair once they are broken, like an earthen pot dropped on the ground. But according to the Vajra Vehicle of Secret Mantra, if you sincerely try to mend a break in samaya, it is like repairing the dent in a golden vase. A scratch or dent in a vase of silver or gold can be immediately repaired, but can you put together a clay pot once it breaks? There is immense danger in being careless about one's samayas. However, when sincerely and genuinely mending them with apology and resolution, then the damage is similar to a dent in a golden vessel; it can easily be repaired.

Most important is the samaya with the guru. Next is that with vajra brothers and sisters. Everyone, both master and disciples, must keep the samayas. When this is done correctly and purely, the outcome is extremely profound. There is a saying among the masters of the past, "Samaya violation is my worst enemy; the guru is my best friend." The real enemy is the breaking of samaya; it can damage the master's health and life. The breach of samaya among close or distant vajra brothers and sisters also creates negative karma and misfortune.

Broken samaya really does have an impact for both master and disciples. It creates unhappiness and turmoil that prevents one from remaining in the state of samadhi. In other words, impaired samaya hinders the training in samadhi and creates obstacles for learning, reflection, and meditation. Broken samaya is definitely detrimental to health, happiness, and all other positive qualities.

"Samaya violation is my worst enemy; the guru is my best friend." This statement by the great Kagyü masters means that the only enemy they could not contend with is someone tainted by the defilement from broken samayas, and that the most eminent companion is their qualified master. Isn't this the difference samaya makes? In short, the best way to keep the samayas intact is through proper view, meditation, and conduct. If that is not completely possible, patience is a strong basis for keeping samayas. It is said: "Don't retaliate with anger when attacked with rage. Don't retaliate with abuse when reviled. Don't retaliate with criticism when blamed in public. Don't retaliate with blows when threatened with physical violence." Be patient even if someone actually hits you. If you can be forbearing in this way, you will triumph over the enemy of broken samayas. Otherwise, if each attack has to be met with revenge, if each hurtful word must be matched with another spiteful word, the cycle never ends. One might think, "I am right!" and say something in return, but the other person will think, "You are wrong!" and counter with more abuse, and so on.

There is an Eastern Tibetan saying, "Words are the well-spring of all strife." This is the main reason for staying in silent retreat. The voice is the instigator of quarrels. No one can know what you think inside, only buddhas and bodhisattvas. But the tongue, being as nasty as it is, [*Rinpoche laughs*] does not want to stay silent, and so begin all kinds of quarrels.

Therefore, the main point is to be your own teacher. When someone attacks you, do not fight back in any way whatsoever. Stay as quiet as a stone. This will allow you to triumph over squabbles. What does it truly matter what other people say? The way of worldly people is to give tit for tat, to respond in kind; someone attacks you, so you fight back. That is how disputes begin. The best way really is to keep your mouth shut as tightly as a squeezed ball of tsampa.

The Vajra Vehicle of Secret Mantra has the potential for great reward, but also for great danger. The great reward is that authentic practice of the oral instructions enables us to reach complete enlightenment at what is called 'the unified level of a vajra-holder' within this very body and lifetime. The great danger lies in the fact that nothing is riskier than the samayas. Isn't this true? Once the snake is in the shaft, there are only two openings to exit from, the top or the bottom. There is no third alternative. Once you take the empowerments, you are caught in the bamboo-shaft of the samayas. And isn't it true that in order to be a Vajrayana practitioner there is no way around receiving empowerment?

Now, there are some people who, while calling themselves Vajrayana practitioners, mistakenly believe they do not have to observe any of the precepts of individual liberation, the bodhisattva trainings or the vidyadhara samayas of Secret Mantra. How can that be correct? Is there any empowerment ceremony that excludes taking refuge? In the moment of committing yourself to the Three Jewels—whether or not they are described in detail—you implicitly receive the Hinayana precepts. Don't you repeat the lines of the bodhisattva vow three times as well? Contained within the meaning of that is the entire body of bodhisattva trainings, in principle if not in letter.

The vase empowerment of Secret Mantra authorizes you to practice the development stage. Through the secret empowerment and the wisdom-knowledge empowerment you are entitled to train in the two aspects of completion stage with characteristics. Lastly, through the precious word empowerment, you are authorized to practice the entire path of Trekchö and Tögal, of primordial purity and spontaneous presence. In fact, once you receive these four empowerments, you have in reality received authorization for the entire path. Having received in principle the entire body of teachings of the three vehicles, how can one claim, "I don't have to keep any precepts!"? To abide by the precepts, one definitely has to observe the samayas.

On another note, for a layperson it will suffice as 'samaya' if he or she can just keep to the ten virtuous actions. But perhaps you want to rise above the state of an ordinary person and become a noble being. All the tools, all the precepts and samayas for this, are included within the empowerment ritual of Vajrayana. You need to take refuge, generate bodhichitta, and receive the four empowerments.

Having received empowerment, you want to maintain the connection by keeping these precepts, even though you may not be an amazingly great practitioner. If you manage to keep the samayas intact, you will be able to experience the six recollections when you roam through the bardo state after death. These include remembering the guru, the oral instructions, the yidam deity, and so forth. Conversely, someone who damaged and broken his or her samaya commitments will have the experience of being shrouded in dense fog and will be totally bewildered. He or she will not know what to do, what to trust, or where to go in the bardo. Such an individual will definitely be unable to remember what counts in terms of the six recollections.

You may not have done extensive meditation on the yidam deity or performed many mantra recitations. Even so, if you have maintained sincere trust and have not spoiled your samayas, you can still be benefited by the fourfold liberation of Secret Mantra in the bardo and proceed to a higher path. These four are liberation through seeing, hearing, remembering, and touching. They are not possible for someone who throws the sacred commitments of samaya to the winds and pretentiously exclaims: "I am a meditator. I have accomplishment." The four liberations unquestionably depend on the purity of samaya. Thus, it is much better to be a simple practitioner who has not violated his or her samaya, even though he or she may not have a particularly high view or deep meditation. Through that pure samaya commitment he or she is able to journey along the straight path towards liberation from samsara and complete enlightenment.

When we look around us, the consequences of people's actions and their keeping or breaking of samaya is not something that is immediately visible. It is quite possible for us to think: "My vows are whole and intact. I have not broken anything. I am pure and clean. I am a righteous person!" If we keep up such a pretense, we are totally incapable of seeing

our faults. Unfortunately, we damage and violate the samayas repeatedly. We need to acknowledge our faults to be able
to remedy them; this is important.

Come to your senses and think well about this. Understand that damaged samayas will hurt you in future lives.
To deal with this issue, you have to acknowledge your own
shortcomings, don't you? Without admitting any personal
fault, it is as Jamgön Kongtrül says in his *Calling the Guru
From Afar*:

> Though my faults are as huge as a mountain, I
>   hide them within.
> Though others' faults are as tiny as mustard seeds,
>   I proclaim them far and wide.
> Even though I do not possess any good qualities, I
>   still pretend to be virtuous.

Most people fall prey to this shortcoming.

Gampopa also said, "When the dharma is not practiced correctly, it becomes a cause for returning to the lower
realms." This is very true. Practicing the dharma correctly
means keeping pure samayas, developing devotion to those
above and compassion for those below, and being diligent
at all times. The most eminent training is to recognize the
wish-fulfilling jewel of your own mind. When you do all
these things, then you will be able to cross safely through the
bardo. There, through the kindness of the fourfold liberation you will be successful in traversing the bardo.

Otherwise, once you arrive in the bardo, you will find
no one to be pretentious with, to lie to, or to deceive. It is
like the metaphor of the 'revealing mirror' that clearly shows
all your deeds. Failure or success in the bardo depends ultimately on the integrity of one's samaya. Those who have

kept pure samaya will, through the above-mentioned four-fold liberation, definitely escape further roaming about in the three lower realms.

You may have an amazingly high level of view and realization. You may have attained a certain level of accomplishment and possess various types of totally unimpeded super-knowledge. But the moment you violate your samayas, I'm sorry to say, you will fall straight back down again. There is no way around that: the upward road is blocked.

Always scrutinize your own shortcomings. Ignore the faults of other people. Keep this attitude: "Whether they are pure or whether they are defiled, it is none of my business!" Be your own teacher; keep a strict check on yourself. That is sufficient! There is then no chance for a single error to sneak in.

On the other hand, maybe you want to go to the place which in the Sutra tradition is known as the Hell of Incessant Torment, and in Secret Mantra is called Vajra Hell. The only way to arrive there is to break your samayas. Ordinary evil deeds, even very negative ones, will not suffice.

You cannot go there unless you violate the samayas. This is the uncompromising fact of the samayas. So, if you want to take a sight-seeing tour to Vajra Hell, first you must diligently break your samayas, because ordinary misdeeds and obscuration will not suffice to get you there! [*Rinpoche laughs*] Then you'll get to see Vajra Hell, with the other eighteen hell realms thrown in for free. [On the other hand,] if you want to visit the dharmadhatu buddhafield of Akanishtha, you must keep your samayas pure. This is the serious truth about keeping and breaking samaya.

Having entered the path of Vajrayana's four empowerments, train in bringing self-existing wakefulness into the realm of your experience. Moreover, triumph over being tainted by even the subtlest breach of samaya. If you can accomplish this, you will journey through the upward directness. That means you will attain the state of complete enlightenment within your present body. Conversely, you may have received Vajrayana teachings but have let the time fly by while totally ignoring the sacredness of samaya. In this case, you will succeed in visiting the deepest pit of Vajra Hell. That is what is meant by no third alternative.

It is said that the buddhas are both skillful and compassionate in teaching the Vajra Vehicle of Secret Mantra. This implies the possibility of purification through apology and resolution. By apologizing from the bottom of your heart and resolving never to commit the transgression again, any misdeed, obscuration, violation, or breach can be purified. This must take place before three years have passed; otherwise, it is very hard. This is the only quality of evil deeds: that they can be purified through apology and resolution.

That evil deeds can be purified through apology is one of the special qualities of Vajrayana. Take the instance of someone who has committed one of the 'five acts with immediate result.' Even these can be purified. In order to purify them, it is necessary for that person to arrange the mandala of the peaceful and wrathful buddhas, to invite a master with disciples in a corresponding number, and to offer them respect and make lavish offerings. Then, in their midst he must proclaim with a loud voice: "I have done such-and-such evil! I have committed the five acts with immediate result: killed my father and mother, killed an arhat, and the rest! There is no one worse than me! Please help me purify my misdeeds!" After exclaiming this, the person must strip off his clothes in the presence of the gathering and the mandala of the peaceful and wrathful deities and make full prostrations while reciting the hundred syllable mantra one hundred and eight times. Then the karma of even these five acts will be purified. This is what is meant by Vajrayana being incredibly skillful and compassionate.

All of us have already entered the gateway to Vajrayana by simply receiving one empowerment. Whether that empowerment was famous or not does not really matter. You receive the precepts and samayas by participating in any ceremony in which the four empowerments are given.

Violating the 'pledged discipline,'—the oath to keep the Vajrayana precepts—is much worse than the 'unformulated evil.' Unformulated evil is what we might unwittingly commit if we are an ordinary person who has not taken any vows or commitments. [However,] there is nothing worse than failing to observe the pledge one has taken, since it is sama-ya violation that truly cuts the life-force of liberation. The samayas include the connection with distant vajra brothers and sisters, like those who participate in the empowerment ceremony a grand master gives to a crowd of thousands. It also includes the connection with close siblings,—those who live in the same monastery under the guidance of the same teacher. Finally, there are the extremely close siblings, the ones with whom we received the teachings on mind essence. That is the most uncompromising; there is no one more intimate than these extremely close vajra brothers and sisters. We should regard them as being as precious as the heart in our chest or the eyes in our head.

The misdeeds and obscurations created through countless past lives must be purified through apology. Otherwise there is no way in the world that they will disappear by themselves. These negative patterns lie dormant as habitual tendencies that sooner or later will manifest in our dualistic frame of mind. We must purify them with apology, which is always possible, as I mentioned when defining the only virtue of evil deeds. This is the purpose of the hundred syllable mantra among the preliminary practices. In this, we apologize not only for the negative actions we have committed within this life and in this body, but for all the negative actions we have committed since beginningless time until now.

Unless we dispense with the dualistic frame of mind, these traces of misdeeds and obscurations remain as habitual tendencies that will recur within this dualistic attitude. They do not disappear otherwise. This is why you hear so often about the need for purification. You can definitely purify them all by means of the four powers in the Vajrasattva practice. Your negative karma may be as huge as Mount Sumeru, but it can still be purified by apology. Imagine a mountain of dry grass the size of a mountain. Doesn't it all burn down when set on fire?

It is also said, "Realization occurs automatically when misdeeds are purified." When your intrinsic buddha nature is free from any veil, it is naturally stable in itself. But normally it is obscured by unwholesome tendencies. Don't the clouds covering the sky make it impossible to clearly see the stars and planets?

It's impossible to train in and grow accustomed to the original wakefulness as long as we are unaware of it and fail to recognize it, or as long as we are caught up in doubt even if we have recognized it. On the other hand, once you completely arrive in nondistraction, the king of all samayas, you transcend the dividing line between keeping and breaking samaya. At that level there is no samaya whatsoever to observe. Until that happens however, there is no way around observing the samayas since we are still controlled by dualistic mind.

The dualistic frame of mind is what we need to be free from, and nondual awareness is the outcome of this freedom. As I have mentioned earlier, these two aspects coexist at present, but as we progressively purify our karmic misdeeds and obscurations, realization occurs spontaneously. Realization in this sense means that the stream of conceptual thinking becomes self-arising self-liberation until finally your state of mind is like a cloudless, clear sky. At this point, since there is no more distraction, conceptual thinking is naturally liberated. This is the point when one transcends the dividing line between keeping and breaking samaya. This is also the point of realizing the four samayas of the Dzogchen view: nonexistence, all-pervasiveness, oneness, and spontaneous perfection. You do not have to try to understand these individually, as they are inherently inseparable. But, up until this realization, isn't claiming "I don't break any samayas!" only pretentious self-deception?

QUESTION: Are we supposed to have pure perception of samaya violators?

RINPOCHE: It is never said that you should have pure perception of samaya violators, [*Rinpoche laughs*]. It is pointless to have pure perception of them because they have broken samaya. You should have pure perception of people who keep their samayas. If they have not violated their samayas, it doesn't matter whether beings are pure or impure. You can keep the pure perception of the one taste of samsara and nirvana towards impure sentient beings and as well as pure buddhas and bodhisattvas.

It is taught not to associate with samaya breakers. You should not even drink the water in the same place as them. If the samayas are broken, there is some obscuration or defect that is contagious, as I mentioned earlier. It can disturb your concentration and make you physically ill. Breaking samaya is the worst. It is more negative than killing one hundred human beings or 10,000 horses. Somebody who has broken the root samayas harms beings from the top to the bottom of a valley. Great realized beings who are not harmed by negative forces or evil spirits can be harmed by the obscuration of broken samayas.

There is a story of Patrul Rinpoche that illustrates what happens when a practitioner breaks samaya and how a wisdom dakini can punish him or her.* Patrul Rinpoche was at Dodrubchen Monastery giving teachings on *Guhyagarbha Tantra*. Jigme Lingpa had two main disciples, Dodrub and Tradrub. Palgi [Patrul Rinpoche] was a disciple of Tradrub, who is more commonly known as Gyalwai Nyugyu. Dodrubchen Rinpoche had already passed away when Patrul Rinpoche went to Dodrubchen Monastery in Golok. Initially, Patrul Rinpoche had gone to meet Lama Shabkar, who wrote *The Flight of the Garuda*, but he had passed away before Patrul could meet him. Palgi lamented that he had missed meeting such a great bodhisattva and expressed his own lack of merit as well the lack of merit of that place.

Patrul Rinpoche continued on to Dodrubchen Monastery. When he had finished giving the *Guhyagarbha* teachings, he was asked to bestow the reading transmission for the one hundred thousand Nyingma tantras. Before he began the reading, a person who had broken samaya with Dodrubchen Rinpoche arrived, wanting to participate. Breaking samaya with Dodrubchen was like breaking samaya with Gyalwai Nyugyu and Palgi themselves. So Pal-

*The following story is extracted from Dakini Activity by Padmasambhava et al., Rangjung Yeshe Publications, 2018.

gi called upon the great dakini Ekajati. In particular, he scolded Ekajati saying: "Aren't you supposed to watch for samaya violators who break the sacred bond? Like a loving mother, aren't you supposed to be watching out for your children? Where are you looking with that one eye of yours? Are you all of a sudden allowing the samaya corrupters to receive teachings? If so, what is the use of your fang? Why are you behaving like an ignorant old lady? You have no power! You don't even know who keeps and who breaks samayas!" He really chastised her.

That very night, the samaya breaker had a heart attack. He was a famous monk, quite learned, but he died from the heart attack. When Patrul was told that the monk had died, he said, "Oh, your eye has seen and your tooth has benefited. You took care of the samaya breaker. Your activity will expand!" Thus, he praised Ekajati.

Now, this monk had been lodging at a guesthouse on the monastery grounds and the owner of the house also got stricken, as a result of staying together with a samaya breaker. Patrul was told about the danger to the life of the guesthouse owner. Once again Palgi scolded Ekajati: "Aren't you supposed to protect the loyal while liberating violators? Is there something you have misunderstood? You seem to be punishing the innocent. It is reasonable that you liberated the other one, Ekajati. That was your duty as the guardian of the dharmadhatu teachings. But here youcompletely lack discernment between virtue and crime. It is a huge mistake to hurt the blameless! You must immediately let this man recover. Can't you determine how to act? Don't you know who has no samaya and who needs to suffer the consequences of their karma?" The next morning that man who had been sick was back sitting in his place, attending the reading.

Understanding Samayas

Kyabje Tulku Urgyen Rinpoche

Yeshe Kuchog states that one should not drink water in the same valley as a samaya violator.[76] Honestly though, we do not know who is a samaya corrupter and who is not. Only the Buddha can know that. One cannot fully measure another person. The Buddha said, "Only I and someone like me can know another." There is no way that we can know who is a severe samaya violator and who is not. And that is not really the point. If we or someone else has broken samaya, we can chant the hundred-syllable mantra and recognize mind essence. Otherwise, there is not much that one can do. One cannot really know who is keeping pure samayas and who is not.

As I mentioned earlier, the old masters said, "My best companion is the guru; my worst enemy is the samaya violator." Many realized masters of the past could never be killed by weapons: that would have been like cutting the air. But the moment they came into contact with a samaya violator, they passed away. Although nothing else can harm them, broken samaya can cut a lama's life short.

The samayas taught in the tantras of Maha, Anu, and Ati are incredibly profound. There is immense benefit from being connected to someone who practices the teachings of deity, mantra, and samadhi. It is said that anyone who comes into contact with a true practitioner will not go to the lower realms. Conversely, contact with someone who turns against these teachings can take you down. There is definitely an impact in relating to either of these kinds of people.

While samaya can definitely be broken, it can also be mended by Vajrasattva recitation and recognizing mind essence. Chanting the hundred-syllable mantra while recognizing mind essence causes all defilements or negative influences to melt away like snowflakes falling onto a hot stone. Snowflakes cannot in any way cover a hot stone, can they? They just vanish, disappear. On the other hand, just walking around in a normal state is like snow falling on cold water: the water freezes solid and slowly becomes a thick layer of ice-encrusted snow.

There is a story from Kham that involves an old guy speaking to a lama. He says, "When you talk about the benefits of the dharma, it's certain that you have no problem. Even this old sinner will probably be safe from rebirth in hell. Then, when you speak of the effects of evil deeds, I'm certain to go to hell. In fact, I wonder if even you might not be in trouble!" Chanting the hundred-syllable mantra with pure attitude and remorse a hundred thousand times will certainly eradicate all one's negative karma without any trace left. On hearing that one feels that there is no problem whatsoever—"Even this old sinner here will have no problem." But when one hears about the negative effects of killing even a small insect, then it is like what the old guy says: "I worry about where you will go after you die, even a lama like you.

There are many details as to what 'samaya' fully entails, including the hundred thousand sections of samaya precepts and so on. All of these can be condensed into the basics, which are the samayas of body, speech, and mind. The samaya of body means to visualize the yidam deity, remembering that one's own form is the divine form of the yidam. The samaya of speech is to remember to chant mantra. The samaya of mind is to recognize mind essence. Those are the three basic principles of Vajrayana, known as deity, mantra, and samadhi.

Concerning samaya with the guru, do not hurt his physical form. Do not beat him or physically injure him in any other way. To not break his command means to not disobey if he asks you to do something. In regards to the guru's mind, do not do anything that makes him upset or displeased. In addition to keeping the samaya with the guru's body, speech, and mind, one has also to keep the samayas with one's own body, speech, and mind as deity, mantra and samadhi. This twofold set of samayas of body, speech, and mind—with the guru and oneself—includes all other samayas.

It is very important to maintain the link with deity, mantra, and samadhi. Where do these instructions come from? We receive them from our personal master. To turn against the master from whom you received the oral instructions of deity, mantra, and samadhi is an immense display of ingratitude. One could also damage the samaya with the guru's body, speech, and mind by belittling his or her words, or by attaching only minor importance to his or her body, or to how he or she feels.

In terms of Dzogchen, the Great Perfection means that everything that has to be abandoned and everything that has to be realized are fully and completely perfected. That is the king of all vehicles. To reiterate, the samayas for the Dzogchen teachings have two aspects: primordial purity (*kadag*) and spontaneous presence (*lhündrup*). Primordial purity refers to the view of Trekchö, thorough cut. Spontaneous presence refers to the meditation training called Tögal, direct crossing. Each of these has two samayas. The samayas for Trekchö practice are nonexistence and pervasiveness. The samayas for Tögal training are oneness and spontaneous presence. So, there are four samayas: nonexistence, pervasiveness, oneness, and spontaneous presence. Because everything is included within these four, these are known as the king-like samayas. All phenomena of samsara and nirvana are complete in this.

These four aspects of samaya—nonexistence and pervasiveness, oneness and spontaneous presence—are explained in the following way. 'Nonexistence'—literally 'devoidness'—means that the primordial pure essence, which is empty is unconstructed, totally devoid of any concrete substance whatsoever. Like space, it is pure from the beginning. The word 'pervasiveness' refers to being uninterrupted in, or undistracted from, primordially pure wakefulness. In the moment of recognizing, there is also some sense of 'ongoingness,' of continuity. This pervasive quality implies unbrokenness, a quality of arching over or encompassing all.

Spontaneous presence is the other samaya for Tögal. From the primordially pure space, spontaneous presence naturally unfolds. It is the apparent aspect (*nang cha*). So, these two—kadag and lhündrub—are actually indivisible, as emptiness and experience. The samaya, then, is to recognize that the essence of your wakefulness is primordial purity free of constructs and that the knowing quality of this wakefulness is the spontaneously present nature. You can also speak of three aspects of wakefulness being empty in essence, spontaneously present by nature, and indivisible as empty experience.

Our essence, which we call 'the basic space of dharmadhatu,' is already primordially empty and nonexistent. At the same time, we have a natural cognizance that is spontaneously present; that is the other aspect. These two are the main qualities. That is to say, in the moment of recognizing how our essence actually is, there is a spontaneously present wakefulness that knows or sees this primordial purity. Therefore, you can say that primordial purity and spontaneous presence are indivisible, or in other words, that basic space and wakefulness are indivisible. This indivisibility is the meaning of oneness, the fourth samaya. The essence is empty but also cognizant by nature. These two aspects are indivisible. Spontaneous presence is not fabricated in any way whatsoever. Once more, the samaya of oneness is the indivisibility of kadag and lhündrub.

Understand the samayas this way: the awakened state of rigpa is not an act of meditating or fabricating, not at all. Once you have fully trained in this and it has become uninterrupted, there is only the awakened state of rigpa. That is the time when you have transcended the division between keeping and breaking any precepts. When going beyond a conceptual frame of mind, there are no more concepts of keeping or breaking. Since at this point experience is an ongoing state of rigpa, the practitioner does not have to hold onto any concept of observing or not observing, of keeping or not keeping, of breaking or not breaking, of recognizing or not recognizing. This is traditionally called 'transcending the borderline between keeping and breaking the samayas.' In short, the meaning of the four samayas of primordial purity and spontaneous presence is that apart from recognizing the nature of mind, there is no 'thing' to do to maintain the bond to, or the connection with, the awakened state of all buddhas.

The moment we are caught up in dualistic mind there are definitely samayas to keep and samayas that can be broken, but the moment conceptual mind dissolves into the expanse of nondual awareness there is no samsara left to be rejected and no other nirvana to be accomplished. At that moment you transcend the concepts of keeping and breaking. Until that point however, there definitely are samayas to keep. Please don't misunderstand this point.

I would like you to be familiar with three Tibetan words—*digpa, dribpa,* and *bagchag*—which are connected with our body, speech, and mind. The first one, digpa, means misdeed or evil action. It refers to unwholesome, negative, evil behavior like stealing, lying, or taking another's life. Digpa creates negative karma, and being involved in those actions does prevent the realization of buddha nature. The second word, dribpa, means obscuration, veil, or cover. Dribpa can be compared to the walls of this room that prevent us from seeing what is going on outside. Our vision is obstructed. These obscurations are something subtler that prevent us from realizing the nature as it is. Bagchag means habitual tendency and is even subtler yet. The easiest way to understand bagchag is through the example of the dream state. Whatever seemingly takes place while dreaming is the product of habitual tendencies and is nothing that we can take hold of. Nothing is tangible, yet everything can be experienced. That kind of delusion taking place on a very subtle level is called habitual tendency.

However, our basic nature of self-knowing wakefulness cannot be obscured, in its essence by digpa, dribpa, or bagchag. It is primordially pure and remains so. As proof of that, observe a time when you are involved in conceptual thought, being happy or sad, planning the future or remembering the past. The very instant you recognize your own nature, it is again seen as being totally and utterly pure. At that time, our nature remains unobscured and untainted by misdeeds, obscurations, and habitual tendencies. After a while, we do again get caught up in thinking in a dualistic way. We get involved with the thinker and what is thought of, subject and object. Being carried away by that, we again create negative karma that obscures ourselves and forms habitual tendencies. There is no point in pretending otherwise!

In order to find our way out of the unaware and mistaken clinging to duality that has gone on endlessly in samsara, we begin with mindfulness. Mindfulness, however, has a definite dualistic connotation. It is like putting a hook in a piece of meat and holding it there. There is a subject keeping an eye on the object. There is a subtler level called watchfulness, which is a mere noticing, but it also is subtly dualistic. Even subtler than watchfulness is awakeness. That is the point of separating *sems* and *rigpa*. *Sems,* the dualistic frame of mind, means involvement with thoughts of either past, present, or future. Rigpa simply means uninvolvement in thoughts of the three times.

The buddha mind, rigpa, is undivided empty cognizance. The moment we recognize that this is so and see this in actuality is called 'undivided empty cognizance suffused with knowing'. 'Empty' here means primordially unformed, not made out of any cause or condition whatsoever, already devoid of any concrete substance. 'Cognizant' means that while being empty the capacity to know is spontaneously present. 'Undivided' means that these two aspects—primordially unformed emptiness and spontaneously present cognizance—are indivisible. They have always been an indivisible unity, and this is what all the teachings of all the buddhas are about.

There is a saying in Kham, "Swing the hammer around in the air, but hit the spot on the anvil." The anvil is where you put the red-hot iron. You may wave the hammer around here and there, but there is only one place to hit, and that is right where the iron is hot. If you hit any other place, you are not going to be able to shape that piece of iron in any way, which is the whole point of blacksmithing. In the same way, there may be an incredible number of details to all the different teachings of Sutra and Tantra, but ultimately, they are only concerned with one point, which is undivided empty cognizance suffused with knowing. Please understand that the empty essence is dharmakaya, the cognizant nature is sambhogakaya, and their indivisible unity is nirmanakaya. To realize this when recognizing one's essence is not an outcome of concentrating or meditating. When simply letting be in this nature, you do not have to unite and fuse together emptiness and cognizance; they are already a unity. There is no 'thing' to do, make, or create at that point. This is the key point of all the teachings of the Buddha.

This is the vital point to be understood, and this is also what we should gain experience in. This is exactly what all sentient beings are unaware of. When there is unawareness of this undivided empty cognizance, it is said that it is 'suffused with unknowing,' with ignorance. It's just like a man who possesses a wish-fulfilling jewel but has unknowingly thrown it behind himself, and instead takes a fake gem in his hand. Although you may make all sorts of wishes in front of it, nothing happens.

There is one single essential point that encompasses view, meditation, conduct, and fruition—one phrase I have now mentioned quite a few times—'undivided empty cognizance suffused with knowing.' This is of sole importance. This undivided empty cognizance is our basic nature, which is exactly the same whether we are a buddha or a sentient being. What makes the difference is whether it is suffused with knowing or unknowing. The difference simply lies in recognizing or not recognizing. An ordinary sentient being is unaware of his or her nature. Ordinary sentient beings are 'undivided empty cognizance suffused with unknowing,' caught up in the three poisons. A yogi, a true practitioner, is someone who has been introduced to this natural state and is 'undivided empty cognizance suffused with knowing, the three kayas. A yogi does not take it as enough to merely have recognized. Without training, the strength of that recognition will never be perfected, and there is no stability. A yogi trains in this until perfection, the fruition of the three kayas.

Do not be content with just recognizing the nature of mind—it is essential to also train in that. The way to do so is as Padmasambhava said in these four lines from *Lamrim Yeshe Nyingpo:*

> Empty cognizance of one taste, suffused with
>   knowing,§
> Is your unmistaken nature, the uncontrived
>   original state.§
> When not altering what is, allow it to be as it is,§
> And the awakened state is right now
>   spontaneously present.§

As it is here means in actuality. 'Actuality' means seeing directly how it is, not as an idea or a concept. By recognizing the nature of the thinker, one realizes the fact that emptiness and cognizance are an indivisible unity. This fact is no longer hidden; it is experienced. When this actuality is allowed to be as it is, it is not contrived in any way whatsoever. Then the state of a buddha, the awakened state, is, right now, spontaneously perfected. All obscuration has dissolved. These are quite impressive words, these four lines spoken by Padmasambhava himself. They encapsulate the whole meaning of training in the view, meditation, conduct, and fruition.

Once more, it is not enough to recognize the nature of mind as being empty and cognizant. We have to train in perfecting its strength. The training is to recognize again and again. The moment we recognize undivided empty cognizance, that is rigpa itself. But it is not fully grown,not an adult state of rigpa. It's baby rigpa. The level of recognition we are at now is called baby rigpa. It needs to grow up, because at present it is not capable of conducting itself or functioning fully. We need to grow to the level of a human who has developed the strength,' who has reached the age of seventeen, eighteen, or nineteen, become independent, and can take care of him or herself. That is stability. For that to happen, we need to train repeatedly. That is essential!

The word 'simplicity' is extremely important in Dzogchen. Simplicity means free from mental constructs, free from extraneous concepts. A famous statement says:

> See the view of no viewing.
> Train in the meditation with nothing meditated
> upon.
> Carry out the conduct of nondoing.
> Achieve the fruition in which there is no thing
> attained.

This statement is incredibly profound, and it is very important to understand exactly what is meant here. It is pointing at simplicity, at nondoing, at nonaction, at the very fact that our innate nature is not a view to be seen as a new orientation that we somehow gain comprehension of. The true view is not like that at all.

Complexity obscures simplicity. In all the other vehicles,

starting with the vehicle for shravakas and up to and including Anu Yoga, there are principles to grasp and objects to hold in mind. There are actions to carry out and results to achieve. But the view, meditation, conduct, and fruition of Ati Yoga transcend everything other than acknowledging what is originally present as our own nature. This vehicle is simply a matter of acknowledging that our essence is already an undivided empty cognizance. Why imagine being empty what is already empty? There is no need to grasp an emptiness that is anything other than what already is. This is the meaning of 'see the view of no viewing.'

Next, 'train in the meditation with nothing meditated upon.' To meditate means to keep something in mind. Do we have to keep in mind the empty cognizance, or do we rather simply acknowledge what is already present? How can you imagine empty cognizance, anyway? It is not necessary to do anything fancy; simply see how it already is.

As for 'carrying out the conduct of nondoing,' in all the other vehicles there is something to do to keep oneself busy with, but here the ultimate conduct is to abandon the ninefold activities. It is said, "Don't busy yourself with deeds and doings." Deeds and doings mean activity involving subject and object that obscures the state of nonaction. It is also said, "Being free from deeds and doings, you have arrived at nondoing." That is the very key point. In this teaching, we simply need to recognize the original state of empty cognizance. At that point there is no 'thing' to concentrate upon, no struggle to achieve.

All teachings are completed in the Great Perfection. The sutras all start out with, "In the Indian language, the title is such-and-such," and end with, "Hereby the sutra called such-and-such is completed." The word 'completed' means finished, perfected. In other words, in the moment of recognizing the nature of mind, all the vehicles are perfected. Great Perfection means that our nature itself is already fully perfect. We don't have to make our empty essence pure; it is primordially pure. We don't have to make our basic nature cognizant; it is already spontaneously perfected as cognizance. We do not need to fabricate the all-pervasive capacity. Honestly, how could you possibly create the empty essence or cognizant nature? They are spontaneously present, effortlessly. Train in this effortlessness and hit the anvil where the iron is hot!

Confession of the Twenty-Eight Samayas *

Padmasambhava and Chokgyur Lingpa

There are numerous scriptures and tantras
Taught by the teacher Vajrasattva,⚬
But in short, having entered the gate of the
    Mahayoga of Secret Mantra,⚬
One should abide by the vajra samayas, the
    permanent pursuit⚬
That are not to be transgressed—observe them
    correctly.⚬

This has been stated in the tantras of the secret
    teachings,⚬
But due to ignorance, laziness, recklessness, and
    indolence,⚬
I have transgressed the commands and dissipated
    the samayas.⚬
I now openly confess with deep remorse and
    regret.
Please forgive me in the state of nonconceptual
    equanimity.⚬

As for the root samayas of body, speech, and
    mind;⚬
Because of weak respect and devotion
I have gone against the mind of the vajra master.⚬

---

*Extracted from *The Ocean of Amrita*, p. 165-170

Because of lacking affection and modesty
I have gone against the minds of my dharma
brothers and sisters.

Having interrupted mantras and mudras with
laziness, I have gone against the samaya of
speech.

The four general, the eight intermediate, and the
secret samayas, etc.,
The secrets that I have divulged, and so forth,
What ought to be secret and what was entrusted
to secrecy:
Whatever root samayas I have transgressed,
I now openly confess with deep remorse and
regret.
Please accept me with your compassion, all-
pervading like the sky.
Let all my defects and faults be purified as I
confess them,
And bestow upon me the siddhis of body, speech,
and mind.

As for the five samayas of 'what is not to be
discarded':
The five wisdoms of desire, anger, and stupidity,
As well as arrogance and envy,
Are to be enjoyed in the unexcelled Secret
Mantra.
They are the adornment of the supreme display of
Samantabhadra
And of the nature of the five families and five
wisdoms from the beginning,

But I did not realize this. ᠄

Please forgive what I have discarded due to wrong thinking. ᠄

As for the five samayas of 'what is to be adopted': ᠄

Meat, feces, urine, semen, and blood, ᠄
Are of the nature of the five nectars from the beginning. ᠄
They are the sadhana substances of all the buddhas of the three times ᠄
And the path taken by all the countless victorious ones. ᠄
While they are primordially of pure nature, ᠄
Due to concepts of pure and impure, and through lack of yogic discipline, ᠄
I did not realize them to be the dharmata state of equality, ᠄
So please forgive me for not adopting the substances of samaya. ᠄

As for the five samayas of 'what is to be engaged in': ᠄
The view of realizing the absence of birth and death, ᠄
The place, time, and clear samadhi, ᠄
Delivering all of the three realms from their abodes, ᠄
The view of absence of meeting and parting throughout the three times, ᠄
The mantra, mudra, and maintaining clear samadhi, ᠄

The uniting of the true activities of means and
    knowledge,⟅
Skillfully taking, in the form of light rays, what is
    not given,⟅
The food and wealth of those fettered by avarice,⟅
And making offerings to the noble ones for the
    welfare of beings,⟅
Telling lies because the view and conduct of Secret
    Mantra⟅
Are not understood by others and are hard to
    fathom,⟅
Cutting the core of the ten objects, the mantras of
    wrathful conduct.⟅
As these are stated in the teachings and scriptures,
Please forgive me for what I have not engaged in
    and applied in practice.⟅

As for the five samayas of 'what should be known':
The five skandhas, the five consciousnesses, the
    faculties,⟅
The five elements, the five sense pleasures,⟅
The five colors, the five medicines, and so forth⟅
Are of the nature of the five families and five
    wisdoms⟅
As stated in the words of the victorious ones.⟅
They should be known as the five family consorts,⟅
But out of feeble intelligence I did not realize
    that.⟅
Please forgive me as I have gone against the
    teachings and scriptures.⟅

As for the five samayas of 'what should be
    practiced':

All that is outer and inner, the world and beings,
    all that appears and exists, $\frac{8}{5}$
Is primordially of the nature of the five buddhas. $\frac{8}{5}$
Although they don't exist apart from my own
    nature,
I have a feeble power of understanding and
    awareness. $\frac{8}{5}$
Please forgive my lack of perfect realization. $\frac{8}{5}$

Mending

Lama Putsi

Although you have entered the gate of Secret Mantra Vajrayana, if you violate the samayas there will be no fruition and instead you will have misfortune. Therefore, when samayas have been violated, a method for mending and purification is extremely important for all practitioners...
To mend violated samayas is 'mending,' and to apologize and perform the cleansing is 'purification.' There are, indeed, the general ways of mending and apology, but they should be embraced by oral instructions... *

The act of mending and purification is comprised of the preliminaries, the main part, and a conclusion. The preliminaries involve visualizing the objects of apology, making mandala offerings, supplicating, apologizing for failings, retaking the vows, and pledging to keep the samayas.

To begin, even though they are in essence indivisible from your own buddha nature of nondual awareness, you should imagine your guru and all the masters of your lineage, the Three Jewels (Buddha, Dharma, and Sangha), and the Three Roots (gurus, yidams, and dakinis) all gather in the sky before you. Then, before all these objects of refuge, chant what is known as *Om Yeshe Kuchok*, a text taken from *The Tantra of Apology*.

When it comes to apologizing for more general faults and failings, you begin by apologizing for all the ways that you

---

*Extracted from *The Ocean of Amrita, A Vajrayana Tantric Mending and Purification Practice,* page 5.

have violated the three levels of precepts, followed by apologizing specifically for having broken any of the fourteen root downfalls of Vajrayana.

If you have committed a really severe transgression, like one of the major downfalls, before making the general apologies in the assembly, you must first confess it to the person from whom you took the precepts. In their presence, you should express your remorse: "I have done such-and-such, and I am really deeply sorry."

It is said:

> Time and time again, exert yourself
> In the ritual of mending violations.

When one of the fourteen root downfalls has occurred, if one-sixth of the day has passed, it is called a 'transgression of period' and thus is an actual root downfall. If up to one day has passed, it is called a 'breach' and thus the person who has transgressed should offer a feast offering (*ganachakra*) of mending breaches to the guru personally or to his chief disciples. If up to one month has passed, it is a 'violation' and thus one should offer one's body, wealth, and all one's possessions. If up to one year has passed, it is a 'severe transgression' and thus one should offer one's children, spouse, cattle, and so forth. After that, if up to three years have passed, it is a 'complete break' and thus one should accomplish whatever pleases the guru without concern for one's own life.

Mending the fourteen root violations through performance of the above-mentioned ritual is called 'definite timing.' Daily mending and purifying all breaches of branch samayas is called 'indefinite timing.' Whichever is the case, it is said:

In a blessed and auspicious hermitage,
Arrange beautiful objects of Body, Speech, and
    Mind.
Place your congenial dharma brothers and sisters
    in a line,
And open up the great mandala
Of the profound Heart Practice.

Gather whatever you have on the new moon, full moon,
the eighth or the tenth day of the waxing or waning moon.
In an auspicious place full of blessings, clean the site and
arrange the shrine objects of Body, Speech, and Mind and
whatever you have of pleasing feast articles. If it is a site that
hasn't been tamed, perform the land-ritual.

APOLOGY FOR SPECIFIC ROOT-
DOWNFALLS OF MANTRA

*Chant with intense remorse for any violation of the specific four-
teen root-downfalls of Secret Mantra that are certain to cause
rebirth in the exceptional hells:* *

It is taught that the accomplishment of a vajra-
    holder
Results from following a master.
So, to disparage one's master
Is said to be the first root-downfall.
I deeply apologize for violating the first.

---

* Extracted from *The Ocean of Amrita,* page 110.

To transgress the word of the Sugata
Is said to be the second downfall.
I deeply apologize for violating the second.

To show anger towards a vajra friend
Is described as being the third fault.
I deeply apologize for violating the third.

To forsake love for all beings
Is proclaimed by the victorious ones as the fourth.
I deeply apologize for violating the fourth.

Bodhichitta is the root of the dharma.
Disavowing it is the fifth downfall.
I deeply apologize for violating the fifth.

The sixth is to condemn the dharma,
To establish views of self or others.
I deeply apologize for violating the sixth.

The seventh is to divulge the secrets
To sentient beings who are not fully matured.
I deeply apologize for violating the seventh.

The eighth downfall is to disparage
The body whose nature is the five buddhas.
I deeply apologize for violating the eighth.

The ninth is to harbor doubt
About the naturally pure teachings.
I deeply apologize for violating the ninth.

The tenth is accepted as being
To constantly show kindness to an evil person.
I deeply apologize for violating the tenth.

The eleventh is to form concepts
About the dharma that is beyond names.
I deeply apologize for violating the eleventh.

The twelfth is to discourage a person
Who possesses the attitude of faith.
I deeply apologize for violating the twelfth.

The thirteenth is to neglect the use
Of the samaya substances as they are available.
I deeply apologize for violating the thirteenth.

The fourteenth is to belittle a woman,
While her nature is discriminating knowledge.
I deeply apologize for violating the fourteenth.

To go into more detail, the first root downfall is to disparage one's own vajra master. Since attaining the supreme and common accomplishments depends on one's relationship with one's master, to disparage or to criticize your personal root guru obstructs your progress.

The second is to violate the words of the Buddha. For example, thinking, "I am a Vajrayana practitioner, and therefore I needn't concern myself with the ordinary precepts for monks and nuns." Turning one's back on the dharma by considering certain teachings inferior is to go against the words of the Buddha.

The third is to be angry with a vajra brother or sister. Fellow practitioners are considered one's vajra siblings. The vajra master from whom one receives the empowerment is like the father, and the mandala into which one is initiated is like the mother. Therefore, those who take empowerments and teachings together are like brothers and sisters, and to fly into a rage against any of them, to abuse them verbally, or physically beat them is to be avoided.

The fourth is to forsake any sentient being, to exclude someone from your love. To hold such thoughts as "I don't care about that person!" not only breaks one of the fourteen root downfalls, but also the bodhisattva vow.

Fifth is to neglect the root of the dharma, bodhichitta, the awakened mind.

Sixth is to belittle or disparage anyone's belief or philosophical system, whether it is Buddhist or not. To have an air of superiority thinking, "My way is the right way; what others believe is wrong," is another way of breaking the Vajrayana precepts.

Seventh is to divulge anything that one has been taught in secret. This means to explain such things as the view, meditation, conduct, mantras, mudras, or sadhanas to people who have not been properly prepared, meaning ordinary people who have neither received empowerment, transmission, nor any preliminary teachings. Divulging these secrets doesn't help such people because they are not ready.

To disparage the body is the eighth downfall. The aggregate of form is the Buddha Vairochana; of sensations, the Buddha Ratnasambhava; of perceptions or conceptions, Amitabha; of formations, Amoghasiddhi; and of cognitions or consciousness, Vajrasattva. So, to disparage or criticize the body or any of its components, or to abuse one's own or another's body in any way, is to forsake the view of natural purity.

Similarly, the contents of our experience and perception are nothing other than the five female buddhas. If you ignore the fact that the nature of all phenomena is utterly pure, and instead cling to the idea that everything is just inanimate matter, then you are actually looking down on the five female buddhas. By doubting the pure nature of all phenomena, you commit the ninth root downfall.

The tenth is to maintain friendships with enemies of the true teachings, those who maliciously disturb practitioners, harm them, steal their possessions, and so on. Being friendly and supportive of such people is the tenth root downfall. This also includes preventing someone who has the intention of creating immense negative karma from carrying out the deed.

Things don't possess the qualities we normally attribute to them. All phenomena are by nature beyond constructs and transcend names and concepts. All concepts such as the various physical elements, horses, yaks, houses, trees, and so on, as well as the labels we apply to them, have no substantial basis. When you look closely at some 'thing,' you cannot actually find anything to attach a label to, and yet, in our ignorance, we persist in just such a habit. We even tend to form concepts about the dharma that is beyond names; hence we commit the eleventh root downfall.

The twelfth downfall is more personal in nature: to cause others to lose faith. This is not just a Vajrayana precept but is applicable to the other vehicles as well. Being a practitioner means that one is now a representative of the teachings, so one should not carelessly behave in ways that will cause others to lose faith or distrust any true teacher. Instead, all dharma practitioners should behave in whatever way is necessary to gradually guide beings, teaching whatever is appropriate to a specific individual, and to behave in a manner conducive to one's own progress.

The thirteenth concerns refusing the samaya substances, including the five meats and the five nectars, during a Vajrayana ritual. For example, if some wine and meat are being used as a samaya substance during a feast offering and one refuses, on the grounds that the Buddha said monks and nuns should not eat meat or drink intoxicating liquids, one would be committing the thirteenth downfall. Of course, if it is outside the feast offering, then even a Vajrayana monk or nun shouldn't drink even a drop of alcohol.

The fourteenth downfall is to criticize women, as their nature is knowledge (*prajna*). In general, all Vajrayana teachings should be understood as the unity of means and knowledge, which comes in many contexts, including the union of male and female. The male has the nature of skillful means and the female is said to be the nature of knowledge. So, one should not harbor the idea that women are inferior or cause trouble by diverting our attention. Also, since the male is the nature of skillful means, to criticize men is also to commit this root downfall. In brief, being sexist is to break the fourteenth root precept of Vajrayana.

In other Buddhist teachings, for example in the chapter on concentration in *The Way of the Bodhisattva*, there is a lot of laying blame on women and presenting a list of their bad qualities. However, this is only because attachment and desire are seen as obstacles to concentration, and the teaching was only given to a gathering of monks for whom women and desire were a distraction. But, if the teaching were being given to a group of women, then the same criticisms would have been made of the object of attraction for women, namely men. It goes both ways.

If a *ngakpa*, one who follows the Vajrayana, avoids all fourteen downfalls, he or she will definitely attain both the supreme and common accomplishments (*siddhi*).

The fourteen root downfalls are related to the four empowerments. Nine of them directly concern the vase empowerment: (1) to disparage one's own vajra master, (2) to violate the words of the Buddha, (3) to be angry with a vajra brother or sister, (4) to forsake any sentient being, (6) to belittle or disparage anyone's belief, (7) to divulge anything that one has been taught in secret, (8) to disparage the body, (10) to support the enemies of the dharma, and (12) to cause others to lose faith. Two are connected with the secret empowerment: (5) disavowing bodhichitta and (13) neglecting the use of the samaya substances. The fourteenth downfall, not to disparage women as they are of the nature of knowledge, is directly related to the third empowerment. The remaining two—(9) harboring doubt about the naturally pure teachings and (11) forming concepts about the dharma that is beyond names—relate to the fourth empowerment.

If you have received all four empowerments, you have committed yourself to keeping all fourteen. When you inevitably do break the samayas, you should go to a master who can act as a preceptor, apologize, mend and repair whatever samayas have been broken, and then receive the empowerments again.

The precepts of individual liberation are like a pot of clay or porcelain—once broken, they cannot be repaired. Therefore, those precepts are given skillfully and very compassionately. The Vajrayana samayas, on the other hand, are like a vessel of pure gold—if dented, they can easily be straightened out. Some minor infractions, for example performing the activities of a master during a fire *puja* or a consecration but not completing the recitation, although minor, are still breaking samaya. The fourteen major samayas listed above are the more severe precepts, and that's why they are called 'root downfalls.' In either case, when you break any of the samayas, the most important thing is to acknowledge it immediately, apologize for it, and mend it fully. If you let one day go by, it becomes an infraction; if you let a month pass without repairing it, it becomes a violation; and by letting one year pass, it becomes a transgression. After three years, it becomes a true break, and if more than three years pass, it becomes irreparable.

However, it is possible to repair most breaches. Making a feast offering repairs an infraction. A violation requires offering all your possessions. For a transgression, the tantras say that one must offer one's children and spouse, and if three years go by, a true break demands one's own life. So, it is imperative to know what samayas you need to observe, otherwise you won't be aware when you violate them. If, out of ignorance, you repeatedly break the samayas, such failings will grow stronger and stronger and become increasingly difficult to repair. Fortunately, Guru Rinpoche in his infinite wisdom provided us with the means to easily repair any breaches, from short daily feast offerings to great accomplishment practices, in which we not only mend our samayas but also retake them.

Purification

Lama Putsi

In the extensive ritual connected with the text The Ocean of Amrita, it is clearly outlined how to retake broken precepts and samayas.*

To repledge yourself to the Vajrayana precepts, you begin by attracting the attention of all buddhas and bodhisattvas, their children, and all dakas and dakinis. The children of the victorious ones include those of body, of speech, and of mind. The children of body are the shravakas; the children of speech are the pratyekabuddhas; and the children of mind are the bodhisattvas.

Just as in the previous vow, you pledge that from now on you will emulate all the buddhas and bodhisattvas by aspiring to attain supreme enlightenment and doing all that you can to generate the enlightened mind of bodhichitta.

Furthermore, you make commitments for each of the five buddha families. Starting with the Buddha family, vow to maintain the three disciplines of abandoning the ten nonvirtues, gathering the virtuous qualities by embracing the practices of the six paramitas, and acting for the welfare of others through the four activities. You also pledge to always observe the vows [made] to the objects of refuge, namely the unsurpassable Three Jewels of Buddha, Dharma, and Sangha.

You promise to always engage in the four types of giving. These four types of giving are to provide material necessities, to give others confidence so that they won't be afraid,

---

*MBS

to share the teachings on relative truth, and lastly, to share the ultimate truth. The samaya of the Lotus family, which represents the purity of the awakened state, is to uphold, without exception, all the teachings of the nine vehicles: the outer vehicles of shravakas, pratyekabuddhas (Hinayana), and bodhisattvas (Mahayana); the inner vehicles of the three outer tantras of Vajrayana, namely the Kriya, Upa, and Yoga tantras; and lastly, the secret vehicles of the three classes of inner tantra known as Mahayoga, Anuyoga, and Atiyoga. The samaya of the Karma family is to perfectly uphold all of the different levels of precepts, as well as to make offerings and perform acts of worship as often as you are able to.

You retake the bodhisattva vow to attain unsurpassable unexcelled enlightenment and to liberate all the beings of the lower realms who have not been liberated; to carry across all those who have not crossed over from samsara to nirvana, namely the shravakas, and so on; and to 'reassure those who have not acquired reassurance,' meaning bod-hisattvas with incomplete enlightenment. In this way, you vow to not rest until all sentient beings have been established beyond suffering.

ABIDING BY THE SAMAYAS

Having already committed ourselves, we now confirm the oath that we have taken by drinking a few drops of the water of the vajra samaya. The Tibetan word for samaya is *damtsig*, which is a compound of *dampa* and *tshig*. In this context, *dampa* means 'sublime,' because, when keeping the samaya, one is connected with the sublime state of enlightenment; and *tshig* means 'burned,' because, if one violates the samayas, one will be scorched by the flames of hell. Therefore, *damtsig* means either to be sublime or to be burned, which is reflected in the lines of the verse that is recited when you take the water.

When drinking this, you should imagine that the wisdom being is present in your heart center in actuality, and that the drops of water dissolve into this wisdom being and will remain there as long as you abide by your original commitment. If you violate what you originally committed yourself to, then something inside of you will turn against you. This is described as the wisdom being turning into an iron scorpion that will eat you from within, this state of self-imposed suffering being none other than the hell realms.

PURIFYING

We now come to the main part of the mending and purification, which has six aspects: (1) purifying breaches, (2) general cleansing for yogis, (3) feast offering, (4) mending rituals, (5) concluding liberation, and (6) receiving the empowerments.

Vajrayana practice extends from the time you receive the four empowerments until the wisdom of the empowerments is perfected, namely complete enlightenment. At present, if we act contrary to developing the four wisdoms connected to the four empowerments, that will impede our development and would be considered a breach of samaya.

The four empowerments are said to be like lion's milk, which cannot be poured into a normal vessel, as a normal vessel will just break, unable to contain it. Therefore, we must first purify ourselves and become proper vessels. A *drubchen, a* great accomplishment practice, like *Ocean of Amrita* contains both purification practices and the four empowerments. The general purification washes away the dirt containing the seeds for samsara and restores one to be a suitable vessel for receiving the blessings of the four empowerments.

To fully mend and purify all breaches requires several steps. The first is purifying the six realms. Then there is a general cleansing of the practitioner, followed by a feast offering and further mending rituals....

[*Here we will not go into those exact methods. For more, please refer to the book* Great Accomplishment, *a commentary on* Ocean of Amrita.[77]]

The *Ocean of Amrita* drubchen is a marvelous way of restoring and purifying all the breaches of samaya that may have occurred in connection with the four empowerments. Receiving the four empowerments actually means being introduced to the four levels of wisdom, or to original wakefulness. Inevitably, the habitual tendencies prevent us from maintaining our commitment in regard to these, and so the four empowerments need to be mended and restored. The process for restoring each of these is essentially the same and involves three aspects: (1) an apology for violating the samayas related to each particular empowerment, (2) mending those broken samayas, and (3) actually receiving the empowerment.

The vase empowerment is like the preparation, and the three supreme empowerments are the main practice.

Nowadays, the four empowerments are all conferred during the same session, unlike how it was done in the tradition of Vajrayana as originally practiced in India. Back then, disciples would first request just the vase empowerment, and then embark on mastering the three fields of the development stage. Only once they had shown signs of mastery to their guru's satisfaction would they be allowed to receive the secret empowerment in which the three main nadis and the five chakras are described and instructions are given on how to do the yogic exercises known as *tsa lung trul khor*. After attaining a sufficient degree of proficiency in these exercises, the guru would examine the disciple, asking them to describe their practice and understanding. Only if a disciple had shown that they had mastered the skillful means of their own body would he or she be allowed to receive the third empowerment, which involves the mudra of another's body. That's how it was then, but who practices with such dedication and diligence these days?

THE VASE EMPOWERMENT

The vase empowerment provides you with the blessings required to master the three fields of development stage. The first is the field of mind, meaning that the practitioner must be able to visualize the entire mandala with all the deities, ornaments, attributes, and mantras clearly, vividly, and distinctly. Next is the field of the senses, in which one's environment is not only imagined as a mandala but is truly seen to be the mandala in actuality—one's dwelling place is a celestial palace, the environment is a buddha field, other beings are deities, and so forth. The third field is the field of objects, meaning that one can touch the celestial palace in reality, and, moreover, when other people look at you, they see a deity.

Here the perspective is of critical importance, for we are not training in transforming something impure into a state of purity; we are training in differentiating between things as they are and things as they seem. In order to overcome our confusion, the vase empowerment allows us to train in seeing things as they actually are. The deities, buddha fields, and so on are all qualities of buddha nature; they are already spontaneously and originally present. It is only due to our own delusion that they appear otherwise, and if you practice faithfully and diligently, it is only a matter of time before you will perceive things as they actually are and actualize these qualities in your own life.

APOLOGY FOR VIOLATING THE SAMAYAS OF THE VASE EMPOWERMENT

When receiving the vase empowerment, we are committing ourselves to regard everything—the entire universe, all beings and phenomena—as pure. We pledge to regard the universe as a divine palace and all the beings within it as deities, all sounds as divine mantra, and all thoughts as the play of wisdom. Instead of maintaining this pure perception, we stray into the habit of regarding things as ordinary objects such as stones, mountains, water, trees, men and women, and so on. Moreover, instead of regarding our own body as the Vajra Body, which is the palace of the peaceful and wrathful deities known as the three seats of completeness, we have regarded this body as just an ordinary human body of flesh and blood. In addition, we do not maintain a state of equanimity, seeing the true nature that pervades all things. Rather than regarding everything as the unity of appearance and emptiness, we regularly stray into one of the two extremes, either clinging to a materialist view of solid appearances or else clinging to the nihilistic view of nothingness. Seeing things in all these erroneous ways violates the samaya of the vase empowerment, and so we must apologize for these failings, for which the apology found in Ocean of Amrita is extremely profound.

Mending by Means of the Torma of Sense Pleasures to Rectify the Violations of the Body and Channels

Having apologized for violating the samayas related to the vase empowerment, together with those taken while progressing on the path of Mahayoga, we now mend the samayas by means of the torma of sense pleasures. Within the Vajra Body are the subtle channels known (nadis), which are mended by the torma offering. The torma symbolizes the universe and the beings within it, in that the torma plate represents the universe, while the torma itself represents sentient beings.

To receive the vase empowerment, you make offerings, saying OM VAJRA ARGHAM PADYAM PUSHPA DHUPA ALOKE GANDHE NAIVIDYA SHABTA PRATISHTHA SVAHA, and imagine "The empowerment deities filling the sky confer empowerment with the precious vase endowed with numerous auspicious emblems and replete with a stream of nectar."

This is the vase that was consecrated earlier, within which all the peaceful and wrathful deities have dissolved into wisdom nectar. You should imagine that they are all present in innumerable forms packed together as densely as sesame seeds packed in a full jar. As the vase is placed at the crown of the practitioners' heads and then some of the water from it is drank, the wisdom nectar confers the empowerment. This is summarized in the word *abhishencha*, which means both 'to scatter' and 'to pour,' in that, pouring out the wisdom nectar anoints the practitioners and scatters their disturbing emotions. Furthermore, aggregates are transformed into the five buddhas, and the five wisdoms are realized. As the sign of empowerment, one is crowned with the five buddha families.

Thus, by having been given the vase empowerment, the defilement of one's body is purified; one is authorized to practice the path of the development stage; and one has realized the wisdom in which whatever is seen is manifest as the mandala of the deity. Thus, one is provided with the fortune to attain the fruition of nirmanakaya.

THE SECRET EMPOWERMENT

The second empowerment is the secret empowerment, which the vajra master introduces by revealing his own body as the mandala. It employs a skull cup filled with consecrated wine or beer. A special ingredient called *mendrub* is added to the wine or beer. Mendrub, originating with Guru Rinpoche and passed on through the lineage, is prepared using some of the original as a starter. Containing the five meats and five nectars, it is dissolved in wine or beer.

The secret empowerment points out that within the hollowness of our Vajra Body are three main channels and five chakras. By doing various yogic exercises in which you manipulate the channels and energies [*prana*], you can ignite the blissful heat and recognize that the essence of bliss is emptiness. You also dissolve the twenty-one thousand circulations of the ordinary karmic winds into the central channel. By employing such skillful means, you can attain perfection in your own body. Here your own body possesses the skillful means to realize blissful emptiness through practices such as *tummo*. Through diligent practice, one can gain some personal experience of what this actually means.

After the apology, the violations of speech and pranas are rectified by means of the rakta of the 'great redness.' *Rakta* means 'blood' but can also refer to the color red. In this context however, it represents one of the three poisons, passion.

To perform this [rectification], you mentally offer all the

vidyadharas, the Three Roots, the peaceful and wrathful deities, the dakas and dakinis, and the guardians of the dharma different skull cups (*bhandha*) filled with various types of rakta at the five chakras: the skull cup of great bliss at the head is filled with the rakta of suffering and thoughts; the skull cup of enjoyment at the throat is filled with the rakta of myriad thoughts; the dharmadhatu skull cup at the heart-center is filled with the rakta of the mind's thoughts; the emanation skull cup at the navel is filled with the rakta of disturbing emotions and the root of existence; and the bliss-sustaining skull cup at the secret place is filled with the rakta of blissful essence. You then request the gathered deities: "May our samaya be mended. May our breaches be mended. May our conceptual obscurations be purified. Please bestow upon us the empowerments and siddhis."

CONFERRING THE SECRET EMPOWERMENT

For the actual empowerment, imagine that "all the gurus and the peaceful and wrathful deities engage in passionate union so that the *kunda* bodhichitta, the support for the coemergent wisdom that is of one taste with the nectar in the skull cup, can be placed on your tongue." Then, place a few drops of the nectar from the skull cup on your tongue and chant.

After that, imagine that you receive the nectar of all the peaceful and wrathful deities. By tasting the nectar, the three nadis and five chakras are filled with wisdom nectar, thoughts of the three times are brought to a halt, and the wisdom of bliss arises. Due to this, the four kinds of bliss—bliss, supreme bliss, desireless or transcendent bliss, and coemergent or innate basic bliss—are all experienced. With the conferral of the secret empowerment, the defilement of speech is purified. With this you are then empowered to practice the path of the great bliss of your own body by means of visualizing the central channel within the Vajra Body like a pillar in an empty room, and so on. Through the downpour and blazing of the inner bliss, you actualize the wisdom of self-consecration that everything is like a magical illusion and the moon in water, and you are empowered with the ability to attain the fruition of the Sambhogakaya.

THE WISDOM-KNOWLEDGE EMPOWERMENT

These days, to confer the third empowerment, the master shows the student an icon depicting a consort and explains that this illustrates how one is supposed to practice. To do this correctly, one must abandon ordinary concepts. The practice of the third empowerment is based on an important principle: recognizing original wakefulness as the unity of bliss and emptiness, and acknowledging that this empty blissful wakefulness is intrinsic to oneself. When the bindu descends from the crown of the head to the throat, the heart, the navel, and finally the secret place, one must recognize the wisdoms of the fourfold joys. As before, you begin by sincerely apologizing for being unable to properly practice and for having broken the samayas connected to the empowerment. You mend the breaches of samayas by means of the nectar medicine to rectify the violations of mind and bindus.

CONFERRING THE WISDOM-KNOWLEDGE EMPOWERMENT

Having mended your samayas and purified yourself, you now retake the wisdom-knowledge empowerment. Here, with yourself as the chief figure, Padmasambhava, imagine that Vajra Varahi in the form of a beautiful young consort (*phonya*) with exquisite charm sits on your lap. This is what is illustrated by being shown the mirror with sindhura powder or by being handed the icon of the consort. If using the mirror, take a bit of the bright crimson sindhura powder and make a spot on your chest.

Then, through possessing the threefold notions and entering union with the consort, through the gradual succession of the four joys, innate bliss is stabilized. The four joys are joy, supreme joy, desireless joy, and intrinsic or coemergent joy. The three notions are: (1) that the man and woman are the male and female deities, (2) that the union of their two secret places produces the major mantra, and (3) that the sensation that is produced is regarded as the original wakefulness, in which bliss and emptiness are indivisible.

The words of the mantra mean the following: OM SARVA TATHAGATA, all tathagatas or buddhas; MAHA, great; ANURA-GA, the great passion; JNANA, wisdom; VAJRA, indestructible; SVABHAVA, the nature; and ATMA KOH HANG, 'me'. In other words: "I am the indestructible wakefulness which is the passion of all the buddhas."

That was the actual conferral of the empowerment. The benefits from doing the practice are now described:

> Thus, by having received the wisdom-knowledge empowerment, the defilement of my mind is purified. I am authorized to practice the path of the

phonya, and I have realized the wisdom in which the nature of all phenomena is seen as great bliss. Thus, I now have the good fortune to attain the fruition of dharmakaya.

THE PRECIOUS WORD EMPOWERMENT

The fourth empowerment is the word empowerment. Here 'word' simply means that through a few words or a gesture the nature of wisdom is pointed out and transmitted. There is a citation from one of the tantras saying, "The fourth empowerment is also like that," meaning like the nature of the third. Recognizing the unity of bliss and emptiness in the third empowerment, the same thing is being pointed out in the fourth empowerment, nothing other than the nature itself.

THE APOLOGY FOR VIOLATING THE SAMAYAS OF THE FOURTH EMPOWERMENT

First, you apologize for not having maintained the view of the Great Perfection of the nature of all things—both samsara and nirvana—which is the view of Atiyoga totally free from any assumptions or mental constructs. This view is perfected through the paths of Trekchö and Tögal. In the following verses, we acknowledge that we have failed to practice properly and have not perfected our practice.

MENDING BY MEANS OF *The Illuminating Lamp to Rectify the Violations of the All-Ground Wisdom.*

To offer lamps is considered the most eminent way of mending breaches of samaya, and so to mend the violation of the all-ground wisdom, we offer butter lamps or candles, reciting an incredibly profound prayer.

CONFERRING THE PRECIOUS WORD EMPOWERMENT

To illustrate the main principle of the highest Vajrayana teachings, one can't do much except simply show a crystal. Nothing more can be shown because our basic nature of self-existing wakefulness is beyond thought, word, and description. A crystal is transparent, which symbolizes the primordial purity, and illustrates the related practice of Trekchö, 'cutting through.' However, if you hold a crystal in a ray of sunlight, the light naturally refracts into a spectrum of five colors. This reveals that the application of the key points of the practice of Tögal, 'direct crossing,' can be utilized. By practicing Tögal, one progresses through four levels of experiences, known as the 'four visions,' and will ultimately reach the perfection of complete enlightenment. Therefore, the main practices of Dzogchen can be effectively illustrated with a crystal.

While beholding the crystal that signifies self-existing wakefulness, cognizant and yet thought-free, say:

Aн̐

Emptiness, the nature bliss,̐

Great power of the unified state—̐

In order to realize the awakened wisdom,:
May the inconceivable empowerment be
    conferred!:
OM SARVA TATHAGATA JNANA VAJRA
    ABHISHINCHA A A AH:

By this utterance, remain briefly in equanimity while
sustaining the natural radiance of self-existing coemergent
wisdom, cognizant yet thought-free, which is realized at the
end of the third empowerment.

> *Thus, through the conferral of the fourth empower-*
> *ment, the defilement of habitual tendencies is purified.*
> *I am empowered to practice the path of Trekchö and*
> *Tögal. I actualize the utterly pure wisdom of coemer-*
> *gent great bliss, and am instilled with the fortune to*
> *attain the fruition of svabhavikakaya.*

The instruction, given in small writing, is to sustain the
natural radiance of self-existing coemergent wisdom, which
is cognizant, awake, and yet free of thought, and which was
recognized at the end of the third empowerment, the wisdom-knowledge empowerment, and to remain in equanimity for a short while. By having received this fourth empowerment, the word empowerment, the defilement of habitual
tendencies is purified.

Just like sugar is by nature sweet and water is wet, the
nature of all phenomena, including bliss, is emptiness. This
is simply how it is, and that is the fourth empowerment. The
mantra [above] means, "May the empowerment of the vajra
wisdom of all the tathagatas be conferred."

Through receiving the word empowerment, the defilement of habitual tendencies is purified. Habitual tendencies are much subtler than ordinary thoughts and concepts. Mistaken concepts or normal thinking are purified by practicing the development stage. But the latent tendency to be confused needs to be purified by the three supreme empowerments, in other words, the practices connected with the completion stage, both with and without attributes. Habitual tendencies are very subtle and linger even after other defilements have been purified. In fact, habitual tendencies are what prevent even the greatest bodhisattvas from becoming buddhas. It is said that for the bodhisattvas who are just about to be fully awakened, only the practices connected with the fourth empowerment will successfully overcome the habitual tendencies.

Honestly, from the beginning all sentient beings are already buddhas and in essence are primordially pure. But not recognizing this original purity, being an obscured buddha does not help much—just like the sun's full potential is not displayed when it is hidden by a thick cloud. Temporary obscurations occur from moment to moment, and as they have various densities, the four empowerments are used to remove them, starting with the most blatant, coarse obscurations and ending with the subtlest. The first empowerment deals with coarse concepts of things, people, places, and so on. Then, the various completion stage practices—whether with or without attributes—that are associated with the three supreme empowerments remove ever subtler obscurations, until remaining in the state of Trekchö and the practice of Tögal remove the subtlest habitual tendencies.

To reiterate, the practices connected with the fourth empowerment remove the final obscuration. When you have musk in a glass jar, a smell remains even after it's removed.

It's very subtle and invisible, but some 'thing' is still there, and it obscures. Receiving this fourth empowerment purifies the defilement of habitual tendencies. One is authorized to train in Trekchö and Tögal practices and to actualize the wisdom of great bliss, the innate or intrinsic utterly pure wisdom. That is the actuality. What is pointed out through the third empowerment only illustrates the example. This is the real thing. Through this empowerment, we are installed with the fortune to attain the svabhavikakaya, the essence body as the fruition, the fourth of the four kayas.

It is only after all these momentary obscurations are purified that one is truly a buddha. Never forget, every single sentient being, without exception, has this potential. Sentient beings are merely those who do not yet recognize their true nature. We possess the potential but are unaware of owning such a wish-fulfilling jewel until someone points it out to us and says: "You already possess it. Why don't you just clean off the dirt, rinse it, and polish it?" One polishes it by living in a smoother and softer manner until the buddha nature shines forth in all its radiance. Make no mistake: this is not an act of transformation, improving one's state from being impure to being pure—our basic nature always has been pure and never changes. Our efforts on the path only remove the obscurations temporarily veiling our essence.

This is the unique perspective of Vajrayana practice, unlike the general teachings of the Buddha where attaining complete and total enlightenment is said to take thirty-seven incalculable eons. Due to the skillful means employed in Vajrayana, if you simply keep your samayas pure, even without doing any practice at all, it never takes longer than sixteen lifetimes to achieve enlightenment. If you do practice, then following Kriya Yoga it will take seven lifetimes; Upa Yoga, five lifetimes; Yoga Tantra, just three lifetimes. If you have the good fortune to follow the path of Dzogchen, then, without hardship, you can attain enlightenment in this very body and life.

Tibetan Source Material

Chokling Tersar, Volume KI,

The Destroyer of All Evil Deeds and Obscurations, This is the general procedure of empowerments for accepting the devoted ones, according to the Pure Gold Great Perfection, the Heart Essence of Samantabhadra. Pages, 83-92

The Sky with Vast Ornaments of Jewel Displays, A sequence of the entire ripening and freeing transmissions of the Heart Essence of Samantabhadra, the Pure Gold Great Perfection of Chokgyur Lingpa. Kya Khab Dorje, the Fifteenth Karmapa. *Here is an abridged version of empowerment manual. Complete manual is on* pages, 109-160.

Chokling Tersar, Volume KHI

Padmasambhava, Chokgyur Lingpa, Jamgon Kongtrul Lodro Thaye, Jokyab Rinpoche, The Lamrim Yeshe Nyingpo, The Light of Wisdom, pages, 67-519

Chokling Tersar, Volume NGA

Padmasambhava, Chokgyur Lingpa, The Concise Quintessence, The Abbreviated Essential Empowerment for *Lamey Tukdrup Barchey Kunsel, bla ma'i thugs sgrub bar chad kun sel gyi don dbang mdor bsdus zur rgyan gyi spras pa snying po'i bcud bsdus bzhugs so.* Embellished with Additional Notes by Tersey Tulku and Adapted by Kyabje Tulku Urgyen Rinpoche. Total empowerment pages 167-201

Padmasambhava, Chokgyur Lingpa, *Confession of the Twenty-Eight Samayas,* extracted from the *Ocean of Amrita, rdo rje theg pa sngags kyi gso sbyong bdud rtsi'i rol mtsho,* pages, 269-475

Tsele Natsok Rangdröl, The Ripening Empowerments, extracted from *Wishfulfilling Nectar to Delight the Worthy Offered in Reply to Questions on the Key Points of the Ripening Empowerments and the Mahamudra Path of Liberation.* Tsadra.org/website

Lerab Lingpa, Notes on the Empowerment for Chetsün Nyingtig, from his commentary, Shechen Edition of the Chetsün Nyingtig.

Appendices

The Concise Quintessence

The Abbreviated Essential Empowerment for
Lamey Tukdrup Barchey Kunsel

Embellished with additional notes by Tersey Tulku
and adapted by Kyabje Tulku Urgyen Rinpoche

NAMO GURU PADMAKARAYE

Padmasambhava, single embodiment of the activity
*   of all the victorious ones,*
Remain forever as the essence of self-existing
*   awareness.*
In order to consecrate and accept fortunate followers
I shall here disclose the essential empowerment
*   condensed to its vital substance.*

This has three parts: the preparation, the main part, and the
conclusion.

THE PREPARATION

If you are performing the general offerings and feast based on
either the medium length or condensed version of the sadhana,
and in particular, if you are performing the Grand Guru Torma
or the vase empowerment, etc., place a manji stand upon the
mandala made of painted canvas or heaps [of grains] and upon

that place the vase of victory filled with nectar. In addition, arrange an image of Guru Rinpoche, as well as the required articles for the empowerments of body, speech and mind and the consolidating empowerment of longevity.

Beginning with the supplications, continue the sadhana, whichever version you are using, down to the recitation. Then open the recitation mansion of the front visualization in the location of the sadhana articles and complete the recitations.

When about to consecrate the vase, focus on the vase of victory, and say:

> From BHRUM in the vase appears the celestial
>   palace,
> Fully complete with all characteristics.
> In its center, vividly present is the divine
>   assemblage of vidyadhara masters,
> Visible and yet empty like the moon in water.
>
> From the seed syllable and mantra garland in my
>   heart center
> Light rays shine out in the form of offerings,
> Whereby the bodhichitta nectar of union
> Completely fills up the vase.

Uttering this, contemplate [the meaning] and take hold of the dharani cord. Repeat the above recitation as much as you can. Then say:

> Within the vase of activity, in an instant appears
> wrathful, red Hayagriva holding a lotus club in the
> right hand and lasso of flames in the left. From his
> body flows forth particles of nectar filling up the
> vase.

OM HAYAGRIVA HUNG PHAT:

Following that, recite the vowel and consonant mantra as well as the Essence of Causation mantra three times each.

If you combine this with the empowerment of longevity, say:

In the five places of the entire divine assemblage, as both self-visualization and front-visualization, the five families of Amitayus are vividly present in a single instant. From their bodies stream forth hosts of Gyokma goddesses, like dust motes in a beam of sun light, bringing back all the essences and virtuous attributes of samsara, nirvana, and the path in the form of the nectar of immortal life. It dissolves into me and the sadhana articles, and hereby I achieve the accomplishment of immortal life and become endowed with its power.

Imagining this, wave the arrow of longevity and sing:

HUNG HRIH:
Amitabha and consort, I invoke your heart samaya out of dharmadhatu!:
Bring forth the power of the hosts of Gyokma emissaries!:
Collect the vitality, merit, and splendor of the buddhas, bodhisattvas, rishis, and vidyadharas,:
And of mundane beings endowed with merit!:
Bring back the vitality and life-force plundered by the naga kings in the western direction!:

Collect the essence of fire and all the supreme
   vitality of the Lotus family!
Let it flow together into the auspicious vase of
   longevity!
Perform the activity of stabilizing our vitality and
   life-force!
Bestow the accomplishment of the unceasing
   longevity of the Lotus family!
OM AMARANI JIVANTIYE SVAHA
OM PADMA AYUR GYANA TSHE BHRUM HRIH

HUNG HRIH
Akshobhya and consort, I invoke your heart
   samaya out of dharmadhatu!
Bring forth the power of the hosts of Gyokma
   emissaries!
Collect the vitality, merit, and splendor of the
   buddhas, bodhisattvas, rishis, and vidyadharas,
And of mundane beings endowed with merit!
Bring back the vitality and life-force plundered by
   the gandharvas in the eastern direction!
Collect the essence of water and all the supreme
   vitality of the Vajra family!
Let it flow together into the auspicious vase of
   longevity!
Perform the activity of stabilizing our vitality and
   life-force!
Bestow the accomplishment of the non-
   transferring longevity of the Vajra family!
OM AMARANI JIVANTIYE SVAHA
OM VAJRA AYUR GYANA TSHE BHRUM HUNG

HUNG HRIH

Ratnasambhava and consort, I invoke your heart
samaya out of dharmadhatu!⁏
Bring forth the power of the hosts of Gyokma
emissaries!⁏
Collect the vitality, merit, and splendor of the
buddhas, bodhisattvas, rishis, and vidyadharas, ⁏
And of mundane beings endowed with merit!⁏
Bring back the vitality and life-force plundered by
the yamas in the southern direction!⁏
Collect the essence of earth and all the supreme
vitality of the Ratna family!⁏
Let it flow together into the auspicious vase of
longevity!⁏
Perform the activity of stabilizing our vitality and
life-force!⁏
Bestow the accomplishment of the effortless
longevity of the Ratna family!⁏
OM AMARANI JIVANTIYE SVAHA⁏
OM RATNA AYUR GYANA TSHE BHRUM TRAM⁏

HUNG HRIH⁏
Amoghasiddhi and consort, I invoke your heart
samaya out of dharmadhatu!⁏
Bring forth the power of the hosts of Gyokma
emissaries!⁏
Collect the vitality, merit, and splendor of the
buddhas, bodhisattvas, rishis, and vidyadharas, ⁏
And of mundane beings endowed with merit!⁏
Bring back the vitality and life-force plundered by
the yakshas in the northern direction!⁏
Collect the essence of wind and all the supreme
vitality of the Karma family!⁏

Let it flow together into the auspicious vase of
    longevity! $\frac{\circ}{\circ}$
Perform the activity of stabilizing our vitality and
    life-force! $\frac{\circ}{\circ}$
Bestow the accomplishment of the unimpeded
    longevity of the Karma family! $\frac{\circ}{\circ}$
OM AMARANI JIVANTIYE SVAHA $\frac{\circ}{\circ}$
OM KARMA AYUR GYANA TSHE BHRUM AH $\frac{\circ}{\circ}$

*Having performed this summoning of longevity, recite the
offerings and praises, the supplication, and the confession of
faults. At the end, say:*

OM AH HUNG $\frac{\circ}{\circ}$

Due to the coincidence of making desirable offerings, the deities in the vase dissolve into the essence
of great bliss and emptiness after which they become indivisible from the water of the vase.

*Imagine that. Initiate yourself by throwing the flower of
awareness. Let the samaya beings and wisdom beings become
indivisible and thus obtain permission.*
   *Following that, offer tormas to the general and specific pro-
tectors, and continue with the feast offering up to the deliver-
ance.*

MAIN PART

*Cleanse the disciples while reciting the verse beginning with,
"Jitar tampa ..."*

Sanctify and purify the torma for the obstructors and continue with summoning, allocating, and expelling. Then visualize the protection circle according to the sadhana text and recite the verse. After that:

> By uttering this, imagine that the protection circle endowed with vajra foundation, fence, network, and dome, and blazing with flames of wisdom, is immense and vast, solid and stable.

Communicate the symbolism. Give out and gather back the flowers, and then say:

> Listen now! Form the bodhichitta motivation aimed at supreme enlightenment, thinking: "I will attain the precious state of unexcelled truly perfected buddhahood for the sake of my mothers, all sentient beings equal to space. In order to do that, I will receive the profound ripening empowerments and the put their meaning correctly into practice!" Then listen while carefully keeping in mind the correct behavior when receiving dharma teachings!

Regarding the teaching you are about to receive:

> The truly and perfectly enlightened one, the Victorious One endowed with ingenuity in means and boundless compassion, taught an inconceivable number of profound and extensive nectar-like dharma teachings in accordance with the inclinations of those to be tamed. When condensing all of them, they can be included within two kinds—the causal and resultant vehicles—as *Kunje Gyalpo*

Tantra says:

> There are two kinds of vehicles:
> The causal vehicles of philosophy,
> And the vajra vehicles of fruition.

This present teaching belongs to the resultant Vajra Vehicle of Secret Mantra which is exalted above the causal teachings in numerous ways.

There were no such words as 'old' or 'new' schools known in the Noble Land of India, but here in the Land of Snowy Ranges, the vajra vehicles are well known as the Old School of the Early Translations and the New School of the Later Translations due to the different periods of the translators.

Among these two schools, the old Vajrayana school of the Early Translations is comprised of the three transmissions of Kama, Terma, and Pure Vision. This present teaching belongs to the short lineage of Terma.

There has appeared a countless great number of different terma traditions, such as the earlier and later ones, but the present one in this case is as follows.

King Trisong Deutsen who was Manjushri in person had three sons of which the middle prince was Murub Tsepo Yeshe Rölpa Tsal, a master on the tenth bhumi. His incarnation, authenticated by the triple means of valid knowledge and extolled unanimously by all sublime beings, was the completely indisputable great treasure revealer and dharma king Orgyen Chokgyur Dechen Lingpa, who discovered an ocean-like number of profound termas that were linked with the tantric scriptures, established by factual reasoning, adorned with the experience of the pith instructions, and endowed with the eminent warmth of wondrous blessings.

Among these discovered treasures, on the tenth day of the waxing moon of the ninth month in the year of the Male Earth Monkey, when he was twenty years of age, Chokgyur Lingpa revealed this terma unhindered from underneath the vajra feet of the Great Glorious One at Danyin Khala Rong-Go, the sacred place of the qualities of enlightened body.

Keeping it utterly secret for eight years, he applied it in his own practice. Later, in connection with a perfect coincidence of time and place, he was accepted by the wisdom body of the glorious dharma king of Uddiyana and consort who bestowed upon Chokgyur Lingpa the empowerments and oral instructions as well as special predictions and assurance. Beginning from that time, he gradually let the terma of *Lamey Tukdrub Barchey Künsel* flourish.

This terma cycle is the extract of the heart of Padmakara, Knower of the Three Times, and the single unique treasure concealed under the earth in Tibet. It is like the great treasury of the universal monarch filled completely and unmistakably with all the means for accomplishing the supreme and common siddhis.

In terms of the sections of Tantra, this profound path is based on *The Great King of Tantras, The Peaceful and Wrathful Manifestations of the Magical Net of the Vidyadhara Gurus* which is the root of blessings belonging to the category of the Eight Maya Sections. And due to the certainty of oral instructions, there is no conflict in that it also belongs to the category of Lotus Speech among *The Eight Sadhana Teachings*.

In short, it is like the extracted essence of the meaning of all stages of development and completion as well as the activity applications of the Tantra and Sadhana Sections.

Its root is like a vase filled with nectar; its detailed exposition is like the beautiful lid ornament; its additional sadhanas and background teachings are like the jewel studded decorations; and its special features are like a magnificent latticework. Thus, it is comprised of four grand cycles of teaching.

In this context, among these cycles, this is from the root that is like a vase filled with nectar, for which firstly there is the implementation of the profound steps of the ripening empowerments. Among them there are the elaborate, medium, and concise versions. For this implementation of *The Abbreviated Essential Empowerment* with the four empowerments— conferred as one based on the torma, together with the consolidating empowerment of auspicious longevity carried out step by step—the duties of the master have been completed.

Now, as for what is your share: first imagine the master as the indivisibility of the three kayas, Padmasambhava in person, the glorious subjugator of all that appears and exists. While possessing such devotion, present a mandala offering as the gift to receive the profound procedures of the blessed empowerments.

Having in this way presented the mandala offering, join your palms while holding a flower and repeat the following supplication three times with the deepest unshakable devotion:

EMAHO!
Dharmakaya Amitabha, I supplicate you.
Sambhogakaya Great Compassionate One,
    I supplicate you,
Nirmanakaya Padmakara, I supplicate you.
Grant your blessings of bestowing the
    empowerments upon me!

As you make this supplication, listen to the master as the Precious Master of Uddiyana, who opens up the gate for wisdom and compassion and grants his permission in these words:

> My guru, wonderful nirmanakaya,⁝
> In the land of India, you were born, you studied
>   and contemplated.⁝
> Journeying in person to Tibet, you tamed the
>   demonic forces.⁝
> Residing in the land of Uddiyana, you acted for
>   the welfare of beings.⁝
>
> I shall now give you the sublime empowerments
> Of Padma Tötreng, the three kayas indivisible.

Next, in order to gather the accumulations, imagine in the sky before you the master inseparable from the Immortal Padma Tötreng, emanating an ocean-like cloud bank of the three kayas and surrounded by an infinite number of the Three Roots and guardians of the dharma, resplendent and vividly present. In his presence, form this thought, "I take refuge, generate bodhichitta, and by means of the seven branches I will gather the two accumulations!" Repeat the following three times:

> NAMO⁝
> I and all beings equal to the sky⁝
> Take refuge in the ones who are the supreme
>   refuge.⁝
> Developing the bodhichitta of aspiration and
>   application,⁝
> I will accomplish the level of the Trikaya Guru.⁝

Thus repeat the refuge and bodhichitta three times.

OM AH HUNG HRIH༔
I prostrate to Vidyadhara Padmakara༔
And to all the objects of refuge in the ten
    directions.༔
I present you with an offering-cloud of
    Samantabhadra,༔
Of offerings actually present and mentally created,
    filling the sky.༔
I confess having transgressed and violated [the
    vows of] individual liberation,༔
The bodhisattva trainings, and the tantric samayas
    of the vidyadharas.༔
I rejoice in all the noble and ordinary beings༔
Who engage in the conduct of the sons of the
    victorious ones.༔
Please turn the appropriate wheels of dharma༔
To relieve the misery of infinite sentient beings.༔
Without passing away, remain for the sake of
    beings༔
Throughout the countless millions of eons.༔
I dedicate all the gathered virtues of the three
    times༔
So that all beings may attain supreme
    enlightenment.༔

Thus chant the seven branches.

Having in this way imbued your stream of being with
the precepts, in order to now lay the foundation for the empowerments by allowing the wisdom being to descend, place
your body in the cross-legged posture and sit with a straight

back. As the key point of speech, bind the movement of the winds with the joining. As the key point of mind, do not let your attention wander elsewhere but hold the following visualization.

OM HAYAGRIVA HUNG PHAT

OM SVABHAVA SHUDDHA SARVA DHARMA SVABHAVA

SHUDDHOH HAM

Out of the empty state, with no focus on
  disciples,
You are the great and mighty Hayagriva, red in
  color,
Holding knife and skull, moving in dance.
In your heart center is a swastika turning anti-
  clockwise,
And upon it is Varahi, dancing.
Imagine this and give rise to devotion,
Thinking that the master is Tötreng Tsal in
  person.
Through the power of such deep longing,
Red rays of light shine forth from the HUNG in his
  heart center
To the realms of buddhas in the ten directions.
In particular, they touch the heart of the Master of
  Uddiyana
On the Glorious Mountain in Chamara.
Through invoking the heart samaya of them all,
The mudras of body, speech, and mind
Shower down like rain upon the disciples,
And enter through the pores of their bodies,
Filling their bodies up, at which point they
  dissolve completely

Into the heart center of Varahi, through which
   wisdom is activated ᰚ
And overwhelming bliss blazes forth. ᰚ

*Uttering this, imagine it and then chant in a melodious tone
of voice accompanied by incense and music:*

HUNG HRIH ᰚ
From the land whose name is Chamara Continent
   to the Southwest, ᰚ
The supreme nirmanakaya realm Lotus Net, ᰚ
Trikaya inseparable, Orgyen Tötreng Tsal, ᰚ
With your ocean-like assembly of infinite three-
   root deities, ᰚ
When I invite you yearningly to this place of
   devotion, ᰚ
Please come through the power of your
   compassionate vow, ᰚ
Dispel all obstacles, and bestow the supreme and
   common siddhis! ᰚ
OM AH HUNG VAJRA GURU PADMA TOTRENG TSAL
   VAJRA SAMAYA JAH SIDDHI PHALA HUNG AH
GYANA AHBHESHAYA AH AH

*Chant this repeatedly to shower down the resplendence. Then
gather the blessings by saying:*

HUNG HUNG HUNG

Dissolve indivisibly by saying:

JAH HUNG BAM HOH

Together with placing the vajra at the crown of the head or while scattering flowers, say:

TISHTHA VAJRA

By uttering this, trust that it is stabilized!

Preceded by this descent and stabilization of the wisdom beings, now comes the main part of the conferral of the torma empowerment of blessings.

In general, there is the recognition of the torma as being a mandala at the time of approach and accomplishment, as being desirable objects at the time of making offerings, as being the deity at the time of empowerment, and as being accomplishment at the time of the conclusion. Among these, here during this time of empowerment, you should recognize the torma as being the deity, and so apply the following visualization:

This torma called Radiant Jewel is, as seen from outside, a radiant celestial palace, vast and enormous, and with utterly perfect proportions and characteristics. As seen from within, in its center dwell the three kayas, one above the other, with the deities of the Three Roots gathered like cloud banks, and the protectors and guardians of the dharma carrying out the activities. Thus, it is manifest as the utterly perfect mandala of the immense magical net of vidyadharas, with palace and deities, who are invited to remain at the crown of your head, bestowing their blessings upon you.

From the four places of the chief figure and his entire retinue marked with the syllables OM AH HUNG and HOH, stream forth boundless rays of light in white, red, blue, and multi-colored hues. By dissolving into your four places you obtain, on this very seat, the four outer, inner, secret, and thatness empowerments. Adverse conditions, misdeeds, obscurations, and obstacles you have accumulated by means of your body, speech, mind, and their combination are totally pacified. Trust that for the time being you are authorized to practice the paths of the four empowerments and that ultimately you are imbued with the fortune to accomplish the state of the four kayas!

Having communicated that, with a melodious tone of voice sing the following in order to invoke the heart samaya:

HUNG HRIH
Padmasambhava, the emanation of the victorious
    ones,
Considering all the people of Tibet with kindness,
Prophesied representatives of his body, concealed
    treasures as representatives of his speech,
And entrusted to the destined disciples the
    realization of his mind.

When conferring the empowerment of the guru
    to protect against suffering,
Bestow your blessings upon all the fortunate ones!
May the kindness of the guru bestow blessings
    upon you!
May the affection of the guru guide you on the
    path!
May the realization of the guru grant you the
    siddhis!
May the powers of the guru dispel your obstacles!
Clear the outer obstacles of the four elements
    externally!
Clear the inner obstacles of the channels and
    winds internally!

Clear the secret obstacles of dualistic fixation into
    dharmadhatu!
Bestow your protection on the fortunate disciples!
Grant your blessings, empowerments, and siddhis
    right now!
OM AH HUNG BENZA GURU PEMA THOTRENG TSAL
    BENZA SAMAYA DZAH SIDDHI PHALA HUNG AH
    KAYA VAKA CHITTA SARVA SIDDHI ABHIKHENTSA OM
    AH HUNG HRIH

Uttering this, place the torma at their three places. Then say:

In order to recognize the torma as being accomplishment during the conclusion, trust that by
tasting this clear and potent nectar—the nature of
the accomplishment, which is the torma-food into
which the deities of the torma have dissolved—it
permeates all your channels and elements, your
being is filled with unconditioned bliss, and you
have achieved all the supreme and common siddhis
without exception.

*Now, in order to bestow the consolidating auspicious em-
powerment of longevity to tame beings, repeat this supplication
three times:*

Protector of beings, Padma Amitayus,$
Buddhas of the three times, Lords of Longevity
    and your consorts,$
I supplicate you, dispel the obstacles for long life! $
Bestow the empowerment of immortal vajra life! $

Having made this supplication, in order to summon the vitality and gather back the essences, now imagine that within your heart center, in the middle of a vajra-cross and amid a sphere of sun and moon is the syllable HUNG, which is the support for longevity. In its nook is the syllable NRI marked with the syllable A.

Due to your devotion to the master, rays of light radiate from his heart center that invoke the minds of all the mandala deities. From the heart centers of the five families of Amitayus and consort visualized in their five places, red beams of light stream forth in the form of hooks and hosts of Gyokma goddesses, as many as dust motes in sunlight. They gather back all the vitality and life-energy that you have lost, as well as all the essences of longevity and merit, grandeur and affluence, and wisdom and qualities of the worlds and contents of samsara and nirvana, without exception. Dissolving completely into yourself, you attain the accomplishment of immortal life. Dissolving into the articles of longevity in front, trust that these articles have become the extract of the nectar of immortality!

While communicating that, wave the arrow with silken streamers. Then say:

> HUNG HRIH$_{8}^{o}$
> Vairochana and consort, I invoke your heart
> samaya ...$_{8}^{o}$

Chant the extensive summoning of longevity as above, or if unable to do that, say this invocation:

> HUNG HRIH$_{8}^{o}$
> Five supreme families, I invoke your heart samaya
> out of dharmadhatu!$_{8}^{o}$

Bring forth the power of the hosts of Gyokma
 emissaries!

Collect the vitality, merit, and splendor of the
 buddhas, bodhisattvas, rishis, and vidyadharas,
And of mundane beings endowed with merit!
Collect the vitality plundered by the guardians of
 the ten directions!
Collect the essence of the five elements and all the
 supreme vitality of the five families!
Let it flow together into the auspicious vase of
 longevity!
Perform the activity of stabilizing our vitality and
 life-force!
Bestow the accomplishment of the longevity of
 indestructible immortality!

OM AMARANI JIVANTIYE SVAHA.

OM BUDDHA AYUR GYANA TSHE BHRUM OM

OM PADMA AYUR GYANA TSHE BHRUM HRIH

OM VAJRA AYUR GYANA TSHE BHRUM HUNG

OM RATNA AYUR GYANA TSHE BHRUM TRAM

OM KARMA AYUR GYANA TSHE BHRUM AH

After this invocation say:

Now, for the main empowerment, imagine that
this vase of longevity is the deities of longevity of
the Three Roots, seated one above the other in the
form of Lord Amitayus. The rays of light shine
forth from their heart centers to gather back all
your life-energy and vitality which have been cut,
damaged, or dwindled away, as well as the essences
of longevity of samsara and nirvana. It all enters

into the vases in their hands, boils, and overflows so that this radiant nectar of immortal life flows down through the crown of your head and fills up your body. Trust that it completely purifies the fear of untimely death along with its tendencies, and that you achieve all the accomplishments of immortal life and wisdom, without exception.

Place the vase of longevity at the crown of their heads and say:

HRIH HRIH HRIH

Lord Amitayus, you who have abandoned both
    birth and death,
Fivefold lords of longevity and your consorts,
Chandali, goddess of wisdom space,
Vidyadhara Padmakara, you who have achieved
    the body of immortality,
Vimalamitra, master of unchanging life,
Mandarava, mudra for accomplishing the path of
    longevity,
Tsogyal, consort who obtained the empowerment
    of the wisdom of great bliss,
Lhasey Rölpa Tsal, receiver of the transmission of
    longevity,
Root guru, embodiment of the entire Triple
    Refuge,
Root and lineage masters of the level of vidyadhara
    life—
Kindly consider this place from your invisible
    realm,

And bestow the accomplishments of immortal life
and wisdom!⟐
OM AMARANI JIVANTIYE SVAHA⟐
VAJRA GYANA AYUKHE HUNG BHRUM NRI JAH SARVA
SIDDHI PHALA HUNG⟐

Through having been given the pill of longevity, the substance of means, in your right hand, trust that you attain the
accomplishment of indestructible life, the means that is the
most eminently unchanging great bliss.

HRIH⟐
By this wisdom enjoyment of immortal life,⟐
The gathered nectar from all unchanging essences,⟐
May unconditioned bliss increase in your minds⟐
And may you forever enjoy the splendor of
longevity!⟐
OM VAJRA GYANA AYUKHE BHRUM NRI JAH SARVA
SIDDHI PHALA HUNG⟐

By receiving the nectar of longevity, the substance of
knowledge, in your left hand, trust that you attain the accomplishment of indestructible life, the knowledge that is
the most eminently unchanging emptiness.

HRIH⟐
All the deathless vidyadharas who appeared in the
past⟐
Reached accomplishment by means of the nectar
essence of the wine of longevity.⟐
By giving it today to you, the fortunate ones,⟐
May you achieve the empowerment of unceasing
longevity!⟐

OM VAJRA GYANA AYUKHE HUNG BHRUM NRI JAH
SARVA SIDDHA PHALA HUNG

Through this empowerment conferral, the inside of your entire body is filled with the nectar of immortal life. All of this essence dissolves completely into the syllable NRI in your heart centers making it shine with five-colored light. The sphere of sun and moon becomes free from cracks. On the outside, the spokes of a vajra cross are fastened together above while it is tied three times with a red dharani cord, securing mastery over vajra life.

At the tip of the vajra spokes appears the mighty Hayagriva holding knife and skull cup. Trust that he protects against obstructers and obstacle makers for your life-span. Imagining this, rest evenly in the innate state of dharmata.

> HUNG HRIH
> All the life-force of samsara and nirvana dissolves
>   into the five elements,
> Increasing the strength of flesh, blood, heat,
>   breath, and mind.
> By the sealing of the unchanging essences with
>   NRI,
> May you be endowed with the vajra life of
>   immortality.
> OM BHRUM HRIH BHRUM HUNG BHRUM TRAM
>   BHRUM AH BHRUM VAJRA KRODHA HAYA GRIVA
>   RAKSHA RAKSHA BHRUM

Having uttered this, scatter flowers and stabilize by chanting the dharani mantra and the Essence of Causation.

Now, in order to bring forth auspiciousness, imagine that the master, the Three Roots, and all the deities of immortal life sing vajra songs with verses of auspiciousness, showering down a rain of flowers. The light of such virtuous goodness pervades and stabilizes throughout all time and space.

OM
May the life of vajra wisdom be accomplished!
Changeless, indestructible, and permeating all of
    space,
Infinite qualities and activities surpassing the
    thought—,
May Lord Padma Amitayus swiftly be attained!

Additionally, chant any other suitable lines of auspiciousness from the extensive or medium length sadhana, and shower down a rain of flowers. Play melodious music for a long time.

Thus, by means of these steps, I have now completed the brief actions for the conferral of the empowerment of the mandala of *Lamey Tukdrup Barchey Kunsel,* the extract of the heart of the glorious dharma king of Uddiyana, the single, unique treasure below the earth in Tibet. Therefore, with the firm determination to observe the samayas and keep the precepts which you have received and pledged, repeat the following three times:

Tso wo jitar ka tsalpa ...
Now present a mandala offering as the gift of thanksgiving for the kindness of having fully receive this profound empowerment.

Once again, imagine that your body, wealth, and ocean of virtues multiply into a magnificent abundance like that of the kingdom of a universal monarch. With the thought, "Please accept as your enjoyment all of this down to the tiniest part!" repeat the following:

Deng ney tsam teh ...

Now dedicate all the virtuous roots of having received this empowerment towards the essence of enlightenment:

Sonam diyi ...

Thus, seal by dedicating the virtuous roots towards the essence of enlightenment.

CONCLUSION

Perform now the concluding steps of the sadhana, from enjoying the feast down to the end.

> May everyone who enters with this key of
>   empowerment,
> Which opens the door to the Secret Mantra of
>   great methods,
> Have their minds saturated with the ripening
>   empowerment
> And be established in the state of the four kayas of
>   liberation!

Having received the command to write this from my older brother Samten Gyatso, a master with a sublime character, this was noted down by Tersey Tulku by means of embellishing the exact words of the omniscient Manjuvajra with some necessary additions. May it bring forth virtuous goodness!

This full version of Tersey Tulku's original text was translated in accordance with the oral teachings of Kyabje Tulku Urgyen Rinpoche, in response to the command of Chökyi Nyima Rinpoche, by Erik Pema Kunsang at Ka-Nying Shedrub Ling Monastery.

Notes on the Empowerment for
Chetsün Nyingtig

Lerab Lingpa*

The teacher should be a qualified vajra king. The disciple should be someone who trusts the Buddhadharma and is a suitable recipient for the king-like supreme vehicle by the power of having purified his or her being through the lower paths, or the disciple should be someone who from the very beginning is a gifted person of sharp faculties. In any case, it should be someone who has only little attachment to the things of this life, but a strong and deep-seated faith in, and yearning for, the essence teachings and the master. It should be someone who can keep his or her samayas without duplicity. It should not be someone for whom the view and the meditation training are merely a fancy, nor someone who flaunts their words and is seduced by Mara to becoming an imposter who belittles the unfailing consequences of karmic actions. The disciple should be someone who is capable of fulfilling his or her master's command.

This is the type of disciple that the master should accept by means of the sublime and wonderful method that combines the essential profound instruction with the empowerment of awareness expression, through the complete and scripturally correct procedure of the ritual involving the right place, time, and articles. Thus, it is very important that [the master] thoroughly sow the seeds for both the ripening and the liberating aspects at the same time, so that the profound method for realizing the ulti-

---

*Extracted from Lerab Ling's commentary on Chetsün Nyingtig

mate fruition becomes effective in accordance with the tradition of the lineage masters.

Now follows the meaning of the respective empowerments, which are superior to others.

For the elaborate, exhort [the disciple] with the vase nectar.

A

To the guru who has reached to the limit of the
    four visions,
I prostrate beyond meeting or separation.
I present an offering cloud of purified mind and
    prana.
I confess misdeeds and downfalls in the
    unconditioned.
Free from dualistic fixation, I rejoice.
While turning the dharma wheel of the
    indescribable,
Remain as the great absolute I beg.
I dedicate all virtues in the space of luminosity.

Dissolve the field of accumulation into yourself.

Next, conferring the elaborate vase empowerment:

OM
In the vase of primordially pure space
Dwell the deities of spontaneously present
    awareness.
Through the conferral of the empowerment of the
    nectar of unity,
May the three doors, and the perceiver and the
    perceived, be purified.

*Repeat the vowel-consonant and Essence of Causation [mantras]. With the sprinkling of water from the vase on the four places, imagine that the outer perceived objects are dispersed into a body of light, the inner perceiving mind is liberated into great bliss, and all the nadis are utterly filled with luminous wisdom. Saying "*OM AH HUNG*," place the seal of nonreturn.*

Next, conferring the unelaborate secret empowerment:

> AH
> The skullcup of nadi, prana, and bodhichitta,
> Is filled with the wisdom nectar of great bliss.
> By conferring the empowerment of great
> pervasiveness,
> May concepts of attributes be self-liberated.

Utter the vowel-consonant [mantra] and A A A. Imagine that through giving the nectar, the essence nectar dissolves into the lamp of the empty bindu in the center of the chakra at the crown of the head. From there the nectar increases tremendously and, by pervading all the nadis, the experiences of bliss, clarity, and nonthought arise. Vigorously hold the vase-shaped breath. At the end, imagine that all the syllables dwelling within the nadis also dissolve into luminosity and thereby all concepts of attributes subside into space. Seal by uttering AH AH AH.

Next, conferring the very unelaborate sign empowerment...

Next, show a rainbow appearing in the mirror of Vajrasattva...

Next, the extremely unelaborate ultimate empowerment...

For the special blessing, hidden separately: in order to sta-bilize at the end of the main part of each of the four empow-erments, the master should emanate a second bodily form from his body, the consonants and vowels from his throat, A from his heart center, and a globule of five-colored light, the size of a thumb nail, from the precious sphere of his heart. Dissolve them into the disciple's respective places and seal them.

Moreover, at this point it is of utmost importance that the mind stream of both master and disciple are pure, so from the outset place persistent emphasis on chanting The Apology of the Ineffable Nature.

Next, enjoy the articles of the concluding feast and dedicate the residual. Sing vajra songs and make extensive aspirations.

This is called 'imparting the oral instructions in the manner of empowerment' and is thus a unification of ripening and lib-eration.

Key to Endnote Contributors

1. Jokyab, Khenpo Pema Trinley Nyingpo, aka Jokyab Rinpoche
2. DKR, Dilgo Khyentse Rinpoche
3. TUR, Tulku Urgyen Rinpoche
4. Rinchen, Khenpo Rinchen Namgyal
5. CNR, Chokyi Nyima Rinpoche
6. EPK, Erik Pema Kunsang
7. MBS, Marcia Binder Schmidt

Endnotes

1. Tsele Natsok Rangdröl, *Wishfulfilling Nectar to Delight The Worthy Offered in Reply to Questions on the Key Points of the Ripening Empowerments and the Mahamudra Path of Liberation.*

2. To reiterate, these seven empowerments are for the vase, crown, tiara-streamer, vajra and bell, yogic discipline, name, and the permission-blessing. [EPK]

3. For details about the *Eight Sadhana Teachings of the Assemblage of Sugatas,* see *The Lotus-Born,* Rangjung Yeshe Publications. [EPK]

4. The term 'upwardly embodies' means that the intent and meaning of the vehicle below is essentailly contained in the one above. [EPK]

5. The teaching cycle of *Lama Gongpa Düpa,* the *Embodiment of the Guru's Realization,* was revealed by Sangye Lingpa (1340-1396) and is still renowned as Lama Gongdü (*bla ma dgongs 'dus*) in 18 volumes of approximately 700 pages each. [EPK]

6. The nine vehicles (*theg pa dgu*): Shravaka, Pratyekabuddha, Bodhisattva, Kriya, Upa, Yoga, Maha, Anu, and Ati. [EPK]

7. Ubhaya, meaning *both*, combines the conduct of Kriya with the view of Yoga Tantra. The vehicle is otherwise called Upa or Charya. [EPK]

8. This refers to the initiation into the mandalas of the nine gradual vehicles according to the system of Anu Yoga. [EPK]

9. A fully enlightened buddha teaches beings in accordance with their individual capabilities and inclinations. Each of these levels of vehicles are, nevertheless, ways to full awakening through the ultimate vehicle. In the tradition of *Düpa Do,* the disciple is initiated into nine mandalas representing the nine gradual vehicles. [EPK]

10. The Three Yogas refer to Maha, Anu and Ati. [EPK]

11. The terms precepts, trainings, and samayas refer respectively to the commitments of Hinayana, Mahayana, and Vajrayana. [EPK]

12. The Four Sections of Tantra are Kriya, Charya, Yoga and Anuttara. [EPK]

13. The six syllables obviously are OM MANI PEME HUNG. [EPK]

14. Tsele Natsok Rangdröl is speaking about the state of affairs in the 17th century. [EPK]

15. "The progressive and reverse orders of dependent origination" means that samsara unfolds when ignorance leads to dualistic consciousness and so forth, while liberation is attained through contemplation on the twelve links of dependent origination in reverse order. [EPK]

16. A belief connected to the Chinese-Tibetan astrological cycle of twelve years named after twelve different animals. The reappearance of the animal associated with the year of one's birth is considered inauspicious. Thus, every twelfth year is an 'obstacle year.' [EPK]

17. When receiving teachings, one should be free from the three defects of the vessel, the six stains, and the five ways of misapprehending. For details see "The Introductory Teachings" in *The Union of Mahamudra and Dzogchen*, Chökyi Nyima Rinpoche, Rangjung Yeshe Publications. The three defects are: not paying attention, failing to remember, and listening with a poisoned attitude. The six stains or impurities are: conceit, disinterest, lack of endeavor, distraction, being withdrawn, and weariness. The five ways of misapprehending are: getting the words but not the meaning, getting the meaning but not the words, getting the meaning wrong, getting the order wrong, and misinterpreting the examples. [EPK]

18. The permission-blessing. or entrustment, is a very short version of empowerment. [EPK]

19. The fault lies in giving empowerments recipients cannot honor. [EPK]

20. The word 'self-initiation' in the case of a master is the preparation for empowerment prior to conferring it upon the disciple. In other cases, it means conferring empowerment upon oneself so as to rejuvenate the blessings, which is also called 'path empowerment.' [EPK]

21. 'Secret water' is most likely refence to urine she poured into the skull cup for him to drink. [EPK]

22. The details of this story are found in Dudjom Rinpoche's *The Nyingma School of Tibetan Buddhism*, pps. 766-8. [EPK]

23. The *Illuminating Sunlight* by Khenpo Rinchen Namgyal, hereafter "RINCHEN", adds: The first of these is the steps for planting the seeds of the four kayas of buddhahood within yourself.

24. The word 'incalculable' is the number ten followed by fifty zeros. [EPK]

25. Concerning the four factors of body, speech, mind, and cognition (*lus ngag yid sems bzhi*), mind refers to the mind consciousness (*yid kyi rnam shes*) and cognition (*sems*) refers to the all-ground consciousness. In the Flower Abhidharma it is taught that *yid, sems,* and *rnam shes* are merely synonyms for the same meaning. The Higher Abhidharma teaches that *sems* is the all-ground consciousness, *yid* is the disturbed mind [consciousness], and *rnam shes* is the six collections (*tshogs drug*). [JOKYAB]

26. As for the Vajra Body endowed with the six elements, the six outer elements are the five elements and the element of mental objects (*chos khams*). The six inner elements are flesh, blood, warmth, breath, vacuities, and the all-ground consciousness. The six innermost elements are the nadis as the stable earth element, the syllable hang at the crown of the head as the liquid water element, the a-stroke at the navel center as the warm fire element, the life-prana as the moving wind element, the *avadhuti* as the empty space element, and the all-ground wisdom as the cognizant wisdom element. This is the uncommon explanation. [JOKYAB]

27. The three supreme image mandalas are those made of colored powder (*rdul tshon*), painted cloth (*ras bris*), and heaps (*tshom bu*). [JOKYAB]

    Instead of 'five aggregates,' *(phung po lnga)* in "brings an end to the thoughts that fixate on the five aggregates," Rinchen says the "aggregates as being oneself" *(phung po ngar)*, which changes the meaning to "brings an end to the thoughts that fixate on the aggregates as being oneself." [EPK]

28. For the mandala of the three seats of completeness, the three seats are: the aggregates and elements as the seat of male and female tathagatas, the sense-sources as the seat of the male and female bodhisattvas, and the actions and faculties as the seat of the male and female wrathful ones. [JOKYAB]

29. This means to attain a status equal, without any difference in quality, to the eighth bhumi of the philosophical [vehicle] that takes the cause as the path. This should be combined with the following empowerments. [JOKYAB]

30. The three profound empowerments are also called the three supreme empowerments. They are the secret empowerment (*gsang dbang*), the wisdom empowerment (*sher dbang*), and the word empowerment (*tshig dbang*). [JOKYAB]

31. The thought of clinging to the deity as sublime form. [JOKYAB]

32. The eighty innate thought states. First, the thirty-three thought states resulting from anger are according to the *Summary of Conduct* composed by Aryadeva: detachment, medium detachment, intense detachment, inner mental going and coming, sadness, medium sadness, intense sadness, quietude, conceptualization, fear, medium fear, intense fear, craving, medium craving, intense craving, grasping, nonvirtue, hunger, thirst, sensation, medium sensation, intense sensation, cognizer, cognizance, perception-basis, discrimination, conscience, compassion, love, medium love, intense love, apprehensiveness, attraction, and jealousy. [JOKYAB]

These differ slightly from the list in *Mirror or Mindfulness* by Tsele Natsok Rangdröl, Rangjung Yeshe Publications. [EPK]

Secondly, the forty thought states of desire, according to the *Summary of Conduct*, are: attachment, unclarity, thorough lust, delight, medium delight, intense delight, rejoicing, strong joy, amazement, laughter, satisfaction, embracing, kissing, clasping, supporting, exertion, pride, engagement, helpfulness, strength, joy, joining in bliss, medium joining in bliss, intense joining in bliss, gracefulness, strong flirtation, hostility, virtue, lucidity, truth, nontruth, ascertainment, grasping, generosity, encouragement, bravery, shamelessness, perkiness, viciousness, unruliness, and strong deceitfulness. [JOKYAB]

The seven thought states of delusion are, again according to the *Summary of Conduct*: medium desire, forgetfulness, confusion, speechlessness, weariness, laziness, and doubt. [JOKYAB]

33. The three types of mudra are karma-mudra, samaya-mudra, and wisdom-mudra, which is a mental consort. [JOKYAB]

34. The forming mind that stirred from the all-ground is the disturbed mind consciousness *(nyon yid)*. [JOKYAB]

35. The dualistic thoughts of occurring sensation. Dualistic refers to perceiver and perceived *(gzung 'dzin)*. [JOKYAB]

36. The five aspects of Mantra: The thatness of deity is the relative bodhichitta. The thatness of self is the body mandala. The thatness of *guhya-mantra* is the placement of the seed-syllable and the mantra-chain in the center of the heart. The thatness of recitation is the repetition of the root mantra, essence mantra, and quintessence mantra. The thatness of emanation and absorption is the emanating and reabsorbing of light rays from the seed-syllable. [JOKYAB]

The person conferring empowerment should be a master with the right qualifications. [This is] someone who as the foundation has the purity of the three precepts; who by means of the path of learning, reflection and meditation, has reached personal perfection in knowledge; and who possesses the great kindness of accepting disciples. [This is] someone whose words of advice have the ability to cut through misconceptions and doubts, whose essential pointing-out instruction can make realization grow forth, whose power of blessings can interrupt impure perception, and whose threefold wisdom can clear the hindrances for experience and bring forth the enhancement of realization. [DKR]

37. 'Preparations' *(lhag gnas)* refers to the preliminary ritual *(sta gon)*. 'The ritual for the land' *(sa chog)* means taking hold of the site. Thus, there are the preparatory ritual for the deity *(lha sta gon)*, for the vase *(bum pa sta gon)*, and for the disciple *(slob ma sta gon)*. *Lhag gnas* can sometimes also mean consecration *(rab gnas)*. [JOKYAB]

38. To toss the 'flower of awareness' means to throw away the fixation on good and bad as to the dualistic experience of self-visualization and front-visualization, samaya being and wisdom being. [JOKYAB]

39. The disciple is initiated into the outer mandala of attributes, that composed of material substance, and the inner mandala of wisdom, which is the ultimate. [JOKYAB]

40. Substance is what comprises body, mantra is of speech, and samadhi is of mind. [JOKYAB]

41. The subtle three doors are the nadis, pranas, and bindus. The gross three doors are body, speech, and mind. [JOKYAB]

The deities of the three seats of completeness are: 1) The *skandhas* (aggregates) and *dhatus* (elements) are the seat of the male and female tathagatas. 2) The *ayatanas* (sense-sources) are the seat of the male and female bodhisattvas. 3) The body and *indriyas* (sense-faculties) are the seat of the male and female wrathful gate-keepers. [TUR]

42. The four circular empowerments are the four general empowerments mentioned above. They are called circular due to the round shape of the four implements used: the vase, skull, mirror, and torma. [TUR]

43. The reader who wishes to know more details, may read *Empowerment* by Tsele Natsok Rangdröl, Rangjung Yeshe Publications. [EPK]

44. Rinchen adds that *abhishincha* means 'fully sprinkling' since the defilements to be purified are sprinkled or washed away, while *abhishekata* means 'fully anointing' since the special capacity for being suitable to cultivate the path and attain the fruition is established within one's stream-of-being. [EPK]

45. This empowerment refers to the light rays from the top of the head of all the buddhas. This empowerment is received by a bodhisattva at the end of the stream of the ten bhumis immediately before attaining complete and unexcelled enlightenment. [TUR]

46. Tantra (*gyü*), statement (*lung*), and instruction (*mengak*) are synonymous with Mahayoga, Anu Yoga, and Ati Yoga. [EPK]

47. A major Mahayoga scripture, also known as *Mayajala*. [EPK]

48. The *Guhyagarbha Tantra* enumerates the ten outer benefiting empowerments: "Crown, tiara, rosary, armor, banner of victory, mudra, parasol, vase, food and drink, and the five essences (nectars); when conferring these empowerments." [JOKYAB]

49. The five inner enabling empowerments are the two empowerments of learning and meditation enabling one to benefit oneself, the two empowerments of exposition and activity enabling one to benefit others, and the empowerment of the vajra king of all-encompassing teachings enabling one to benefit both oneself and others. [JOKYAB]

50. The yogic discipline of having equalized conduct and insight means, according to Khenpo Könchok Mönlam, to be able to act with pure perception as the outcome of having perfected the practices connected with the first empowerment. [EPK]

51. Scripture (*mdo*) here refers to the Anu Yoga just mentioned, and not to the sutras of the causal philosophical vehicles. [EPK]

    The 831 complex aspects are counted by the number of empowerment articles. [JOKYAB]

52. The four empowerments of the outer, the inner, the sadhana, and the secret are included within the four rivers of empowerment: the outer empowerment river of the water of Tantra, the inner empowerment river of mastery, the sadhana empowerment river of renown, and the secret empowerment river of perfection. The empowerment ritual for the *Embodiment Scripture* contains more extensive details of these. [JOKYAB]

53. The Sadhana Section is one of the two aspects of Mahayoga, the other being the Tantra Section [EPK]

54. The title of an Anuttara Yoga tantra. [EPK]

55. The title of a Mahayoga tantra. [EPK]

56. *Kunzang Tuktig* is a terma treasure of Padmasambahva, revealed by Chokgyur Lingpa. It a full Dzogchen cycle with a sadhana of the hundred peaceful and wrathful deities. [MBS]

57. "Because of weak respect and devotion
    I have gone against the mind of the vajra master.⁸" Extracted from *the Ocean of Amrita.*

58. Because of lacking affection and modesty, I have gone against the minds of my dharma brothers and sisters.⁸

59. For the details of the [precepts, trainings, and samayas of] Pratimoksha, Bodhisattva, and Mantra [teachings], look in the *Three Precepts,* the *Domsum* (*sdom gsum*). [JOKYAB]

    English title *Perfect Conduct, Ascertaining the Three Vows,* by Ngari Panchen, Pema Wangyi Gyalpo, and commentary by His Holiness Dudjom Rinpoche. Wisdom Publications, Boston, 1996. Translated by Khenpo Gyurme Samdrub and Sangye Khandro. [EPK]

60. The three vajra-secrets refer to Vajra Body, Vajra Speech, and Vajra Mind. [CNR]

61. One literal meaning of *damtsig*, the Tibetan word for samaya, is sacred (*dam*) word (*tshig*). [CNR]

62. The other literal meaning of samaya is 'bound' (*dam*) or 'burned' (*tshig*). [EPK]

    [Rinchen] adds that samaya primarily depends on the pure or impure frame of mind, as the *Extensive [Scripture]* says:

    That which is known as samaya
    Does not exist somewhere else.
    Your own stream of mind is the samaya.

63. To summarize the general, special, and supreme samayas: the general samayas are the trainings of individual liberation, bodhisattvas, and Mantra, which should be guarded as one's heart. The special samayas are the common samayas of the five families of Anuttara Mantra as well as the root and branch samayas, which should be guarded as the blood in one's heart. The supreme samayas are twenty described through analogies, such as not breaking the command of the vajra master, and so forth, which should be guarded as carefully as one's life-force. [DKR]

64. The eight sets of individual liberation, *pratimoksha*, are: 1) the eight fasting vows, taken for one day only; 2) and 3) the five vows of laymen and laywomen; 4) and 5) the vows of male and female novices; 6) additional vows taken by probationer nuns as a step towards becoming full nuns; 7) the discipline of the full nun, *bhikshuni*; 8) that of the full monk, *bhikshu*. [EPK]

    For the bodhisattva trainings within the traditions of the two chariots of Nagarjuna and Asanga, see: *Light of Wisdom* Vol. I, note 247. [EPK]

65. The special samayas are taught exclusively in the context of Unexcelled Mantra. When a yogi possesses the confidence of realized training such as being able to revive the dead, has received permission from the yidam deity and his master, and is endowed with a special compassionate motivation, to carry out these samayas in a literal way for the welfare of others is the samaya of the development stage of expedient meaning. When a practitioner does not possess

these, he or she applies the four types of intent, having transposed the literal meaning, and this is the special quality of connecting the completion stage to the samayas of the higher empowerments. Thus, they are known as 'special.'

When explaining these special samayas, to 'take life,' which is the samaya of the vajra family, is of several types. On the outer level, it means to deliver the ten objects that are enemies of the Buddhadharma by means of 'direct action.' On the inner level, it means to kill the pranas in the sense of interrupting within the central channel the circulation of the pranas in the left and right channels by means of the vase-practice, and finally stabilize the prana-mind in the *ushnika*. On the thatness level, it means to kill the thinking in the sense of composing yourself evenly in the thoughtfree wakefulness and thereby ensuring that the conceptualizing of perceiver and perceived does not arise.

'To take what is not given,' which is the samaya of the ratna family, on the outer level means to take wealth from miserly people, giving it to the poor and needy, and inspiring a generous attitude in the people from whom you took. Alternatively, it means being generous with wealth and enjoyments which you have magnetized by the power of Secret Mantra. On the inner level, it means to magnetize maidens of the types of *deva*, human, *yaksha*, and so forth, for the sake of generating the wisdom of great bliss. Or, it means to take – without being given – the elixir of the queen by means of the power of prana. On the thatness level, it refers to the ultimate queen who is the knowledge of emptiness, and to taking what is not given by anyone else, namely the attainment of realization by means of personally training in the samadhi of shamatha and vipashyana.

To engage in sexual relationship with a consort, which is taught to be the samaya of the padma family, on the outer level means the karma mudra who is an actual consort; on the inner level the dharma-mudra who is a mental consort; as well as tummo which is the samaya mudra. These three are taught for the sake of generating the example wisdom of the melting bliss. On the thatness level, it means to compose yourself evenly in the mahamudra, the original and coemergent wisdom.

To utter falsehood, which is taught to be the samaya of the karma family, on the outer level means to lie in order to save other's lives, and so forth. On the inner level, it means to teach in accordance with the dispositions and faculties of those to be tamed. On the thatness level, it means, while self and sentient beings have no true existence, to make statements that are devoid of truth such as saying, "I will liberate all sentient beings from samsara!" [RINCHEN] more details about the five meats, nectars, alcohol, etc.

66. See the section on the paramita of discipline in *Light of Wisdom* Vol. I, Chapter 13. [EPK]

67. See *Light of Wisdom* Vol. I, Chapter 13 on the section of the paramita of generosity. [EPK].

68. The outer, inner and secret aspects can also refer to the three aspects that comprise the nine vehicles: the outer vehicles of directing the origin [of suffering]; the inner vehicles of insightful austerity; and the secret vehicles of commanding means. [RINCHEN]

   The outer are the vehicles of shravakas, pratyekabuddhas, and bodhisattvas; the inner are the vehicles of Kriya, Ubhaya, and Yoga; and the secret are the vehicles of Maha, Anu, and Ati. [CNR]

69. The actions of offering are the outer, inner and innermost offerings as well as torma, fire-puja, and so forth. [RINCHEN]

70. Among the samayas for the karma family, to explain the meaning of guiding further and so forth: According to the person of lesser capacity, to deliver to the higher realms all those who have not been delivered from the lower realms. According to the person of medium capacity, to free into peace [nirvana] all those who have not been freed from the ocean of existence. According to the person of greater capacity, to confirm in the Mahayana all those who have not been confirmed with peace, and to establish in transcendence to buddhahood all the bodhisattvas who have attained the bhumis but have not fully reached the transcendence [nirvana] that dwells in neither existence nor peace. [JOKYAB]

71. The gross three doors are delivered by the melting bliss of the development stage. The subtle nadis, pranas and bindus are freed by the melting bliss of the completion stage with attributes. The extremely subtle defilements of the three experiences are confirmed

by the melting bliss of the *phonya*. The most subtle three doors, the identity of the essences of the six elements, are transcended into the three vajras by the completion stage without attributes. These four are taught to be the progressive stages of the four empowerments. [JOKYAB]

72. The six periods of day and night. Khenpo Könchok Mönlam says that it was the Indian tradition to do six sessions within a twenty-four hour duration, while in Tibet four sessions were more popular. Tsikey Chokling Rinpoche says that they mean three during the day and three during the night. Sometimes a period is defined as three hours; sometimes two before noon, two after noon, and two during the early and the last part of the night. [EPK]

73. The aggregates, elements, sense-objects, sense-faculties, and colors. [EPK]

74. The ten objects (*zhing bcu*) are described in the *Bright Effulgence*:

The enemy of the Three Jewels, and of the master,

The samaya violator, and the malicious,

The samaya enemy with a wicked character,

The one suitable to include, and who harms everyone,

And the three lower realms, these ten

Should be apprehended by all yogis. [JOKYAB]

75. The essences of the five aggregates are defiling [leaking] outwardly through the five sense-doors due to the circumstance of coarse desire and anger and hence they should be bound to be undefiling [non-leaking]. [JOKYAB]

76. *Yeshe Kuchog* is an apology chant combined with the peaceful and wrathful deities. It belongs to the *Tantra of Immaculate Apology*. A translation is included in the feast offering for *Kunzang Tuktig*. [EPK]

77. Padmasambhava, Chokgyur Lingpa, & others, *Great Accomplishment*, Rangjung Yeshe Publications. [MBS]